AF394355

ISBN: 978 1 83632 083 8
Editor: Mark Ayton
Senior editor, specials: Roger Mortimer
Email: roger.mortimer@keypublishing.com
Cover Design: Steve Donovan
Design: SJmagic DESIGN SERVICES, India
Advertising Sales Manager: Sam Clark
Email: sam.clark@keypublishing.com
Tel: 01780 755131
Advertising Production:
Becky Antoniades
Email:
Rebecca.antoniades@keypublishing.com

SUBSCRIPTION/MAIL ORDER
Key Publishing Ltd, PO Box 300, Stamford,
Lincs, PE9 1NA
Tel: 01780 480404
Subscriptions email:
subs@keypublishing.com
Mail Order email:
orders@keypublishing.com
Website: www.keypublishing.com/shop

PUBLISHING
Group CEO and Publisher: Adrian Cox

Published by
Key Publishing Ltd, PO Box 100,
Stamford, Lincs, PE9 1XQ
Tel: 01780 755131
Website: www.keypublishing.com

PRINTING
Precision Colour Printing Ltd, Haldane,
Halesfield 1, Telford, Shropshire. TF7 4QQ

DISTRIBUTION
Seymour Distribution Ltd, 2 Poultry
Avenue, London, EC1A 9PU
Enquiries Line: 02074 294000.

We are unable to guarantee the bona
fides of any of our advertisers. Readers
are strongly recommended to take their
own precautions before parting with any
information or item of value, including,
but not limited to money, manuscripts,
photographs, or personal information in
response to any advertisements within this
publication.

CITIZEN AIRMEN

ON DUTY SINCE 1908

An overview of the heritage and chronological history of the ANG as compiled by the National Guard Bureau's history office.

ALTHOUGH THE AIR National Guard was not established as a separate reserve component of the US Air Force until September 18, 1947, National Guard aviators have played significant roles in all of America's wars and most of its major contingencies since World War One. They have also aided their country in coping with natural disasters and civil unrest since the mid-1920s.

Mexican Border Crisis

In November 1915, Captain Raynal Cawthorne Bolling organised and took command of a unit that became the 1st Aero Company, New York National Guard. It is recognised as the ANG's oldest unit and its lineage is carried by the 102nd Rescue Squadron, New York ANG. On July 13, 1916, the 1st Aero Company mobilised during the border crisis with Mexico. It trained at Mineola Field, New York, where Bolling's unit was joined by the 2nd Aero Company of Buffalo and 12 officers from other states. Both air units remained at Mineola throughout the crisis.

World War One

Bolling's experience at Mineola convinced him that aviation would never succeed in the National Guard. Probably because of his recommendations, the War Department decided that it would not mobilise air units during World War One. Instead, individual Guard volunteers provided a pool from which the Army could draw aviators. They were required to leave the Guard and enter the Signal Corps Reserve if they wished to fly in the war.

Some former Guardsmen, including Colonel Bolling and Major Reuben Fleet of Washington state, occupied senior Air Service positions. Guardsmen also played prominent roles in air operations in France. On April 14, 1918, Tennessee Guardsman Reed Chambers flew with Eddie Rickenbacker and David Peterson of the 94th Pursuit Squadron from Villeneuve, France, on the first combat mission ever ordered by an American commander of a US squadron. At least four Guardsmen – Chambers, Field Kindley (Kansas), Reed Landis (Illinois) and Martinus Stenseth (Minnesota) – became aces. Second Lieutenant Erwin R Bleckley of Kansas was awarded the Congressional Medal of Honor posthumously for his heroism as an aerial observer.

Observation Aviation

After World War One, National Guard aviation was placed on a permanent basis despite the initial opposition of the Army's General Staff. During the interwar period, 29 Guard observation squadrons were formed. Their pilots, including Captain Charles A Lindbergh of Missouri's 110th Observation Squadron, concentrated on honing their flying skills and supporting ground force training. Guard airmen also participated in state missions. For instance, Arkansas' 154th Observation Squadron flew some 20,000 miles carrying supplies and relief workers during the floods that ravaged that state in 1927.

World War Two

During 1940-1941, approximately 4,800 experienced National Guard aviation

Above: **Two F-106A Delta Dart fighters assigned to New Jersey ANG's 177th Fighter Interceptor Group in flight over the Atlantic Ocean off the coast of New Jersey.** US Air National Guard

personnel were mobilised from their observation squadrons. They provided a significant augmentation of the US Army's rapidly expanding air arm during a critical period.

Most Guard air units were stripped of many key personnel. They were re-equipped with more modern aircraft. Some of the early squadrons maintained a degree of unit integrity and cohesion, but most lost their character and identity as Guard organisations. Before V-J Day, the Army Air Force (AAF) disbanded or inactivated nine of those squadrons. The surviving units were transformed from observation organisations into reconnaissance, liaison, fighter, and bombardment squadrons and served in every major combat theatre during the war.

The most significant wartime contribution of National Guard aviators was to train and lead the large numbers of volunteer airmen who had entered the AAF during World War Two. That role was epitomised by Lieutenant Colonel Addison Baker, a Guardsman from Akron, Ohio. On August 1, 1943, Baker commanded the AAF's 93rd Heavy Bombardment Group on a daring but ill-fated low-level attack against enemy oil refineries at Ploesti, Romania. Baker was posthumously awarded the Medal of Honor for his heroic leadership.

Korean War

The Korean War was a turning point for the ANG. Some 45,000 guardsmen – 80% of the force – were mobilised. That call-up exposed the weaknesses of all US military reserve programmes, including the ANG. Once in federal service, 66 of the ANG's 92 flying squadrons, along with numerous support units, proved to be unprepared for combat. Many key guardsmen were used as fillers elsewhere in the USAF. It took three to six months for some ANG units to become combat-ready; some never did. Eventually, they made substantial contributions to the war effort and the Air Force's global build-up.

In the Far East, the ANG's 136th and 116th Fighter Bomber Wings compiled excellent combat records flying F-84s. Guardsmen flew 39,530 combat sorties and destroyed 39 enemy aircraft, but 101 of them were either killed or declared missing in action during the conflict. Four guardsmen – Captains Robert Love (California), Clifford Jolley (Utah) and Robinson Risner (Oklahoma), plus Major James Hagerstrom (Texas) – became aces. Largely because of the Korean War experience, senior ANG and Air Force leaders became seriously committed to building the ANG as an effective reserve component.

The Bay of Pigs

On April 17, 1961, a force of Cuban exiles, trained and equipped by the Central Intelligence Agency (CIA), invaded their homeland at the Bay of Pigs in an ill-judged attempt to bring down the communist government of President Fidel Castro. Eighty guardsmen, serving as civilian volunteers, trained the exiles to fly old B-26 bombers and transports.

Berlin Crisis

On August 30, 1961, President John F Kennedy ordered 148,000 guardsmen and reservists to active duty in response to Soviet moves to cut off allied access to Berlin. The ANG's share of that mobilisation was 21,067 individuals. ANG units deployed in October included 18 tactical fighter squadrons, four reconnaissance squadrons, six air transport squadrons and a tactical control group. On November 1, the USAF called up three more ANG fighter interceptor squadrons.

In late October and early November, eight of the tactical fighter units flew to Europe with their 216 aircraft in Operation Stair Step, the largest jet deployment in the ANG's history. Because of their short range, 60 ANG F-104 interceptors were airlifted to Europe in late November. The United States Air Forces in Europe lacked spare parts needed for the ANG's ageing F-84s and F-86s. Some units had been trained to deliver tactical nuclear weapons, not conventional bombs, and bullets, so had to be retrained for conventional missions once they arrived on the continent. Most mobilised guardsmen remained in the US.

Operation Stair Step

In September 1961, 28 ANG and five Air Force Reserve flying units and a tactical control group were ordered to report for active duty on October 1. The ANG force included 18 tactical fighter squadrons, four tactical reconnaissance squadrons, six C-97-equipped air transport squadrons and one tactical control group, plus their supporting elements, along with five C-124 troop carrier squadrons recalled from the Air Force Reserve.

Three ANG F-104 fighter-interceptor units – from Knoxville in Tennessee, Phoenix in Arizona and McEntire (then Congaree) ANG Base in South Carolina – joined the force a month later. A few days afterwards, their 60 planes were airlifted to Europe in the bays of C-124 Globemaster transport aircraft.

The tactical fighter units included the 101st from Boston, Massachusetts, the 131st from Westfield, Massachusetts, and the 138th from Syracuse, New York, all flying the F-86H Sabre. Units equipped with the F-84F Thunderstreak included the 119th from Atlantic City, New Jersey, the 141st from McGuire Air Force Base, New Jersey, the 149th from Richmond, Virginia, the 162nd from Springfield, Ohio, the 164th from Mansfield, Ohio, the 166th from Lockbourne Air Force Base, Ohio, the 112th from Toledo, Ohio, the 113th from Terre Haute, Indiana, the 163rd from Fort Wayne, Indiana, the 110th from St Louis, Missouri, the 169th from Peoria, Illinois, and the 170th from Springfield, Illinois. F-100 Super Sabre units included the 120th from Denver, Colorado, the 121st from Andrews Air Force Base, Maryland, and the 136th from Niagara Falls, New York. RF-84F Thunderflash squadrons were the 106th from Birmingham, Alabama, the 153d from Meridian, Mississippi, the 160th from Montgomery, Alabama, and the 184th from Fort Smith, Arkansas. C-97 Stratofreighter squadrons included the 109th from Minneapolis-St. Paul, Minnesota, the 133d from Manchester, New Hampshire, the 139th from Schenectady, New York, the 115th and

195th from Van Nuys, California, and the 125th from Tulsa, Oklahoma. The 152nd Tactical Control Group from Roslyn, Long Island, New York, included units from Connecticut, Massachusetts, Ohio, Pennsylvania, and Rhode Island. The Air Force Reserve C-97-equipped units were the 78th Troop Carrier Squadron from Barksdale Air Force Base, Louisiana, the 303rd and 304th from Richards-Gebaur Air Force Base, Missouri, the 305th from Tinker Air Force Base, Oklahoma, and the 77th from Donaldson Air Force Base, South Carolina.

Although most pilots were combat-ready, they found new demands on their skills on the bombing ranges, in rocketry and in gunnery. They flew long-range navigational missions and practical cruise control. The aircrews were immersed in intelligence briefings, survival training and lectures on air-ground operations. Specialists from the Air Force Survival School at Stead Air Force Base, Nevada, and from TAC's Air-Ground Operations School at Keesler Air Force Base, Mississippi, visited almost every unit.

Left: **In 1959, Georgia Air National Guard's 116th Air Defense Wing received the F-86L Sabre. This photo depicts F-86L Sabres of the 128th Fighter Squadron at 25,000ft over North Georgia.** Georgia National Guard Archives

Below: **F-47N Thunderbolts assigned to Massachusetts ANG's 101st Fighter Squadron at Boston-Logon Airport in 1949.** US Air Force

Above: **F-104A Starfighter 60834 assigned to Tennessee ANG's 151st Fighter Interceptor Squadron based at Knoxville. The unit was one of three that deployed to Europe in 1961 under Operation Stair Step.** US Air National Guard

Left: **Two F-102A Delta Dagger fighters assigned to Texas ANG's 147th Fighter Interceptor Group.** US Air National Guard

Pilots slated for the deployment not only had to be fitted with rubberised anti-exposure suits, but also had to leap awkwardly into swimming pools to make sure the suits didn't leak. In addition, the maintenance crews in the ANG had to remove Guard insignia and replace them with USAF titles, while the big anti-buzzing tail numbers had to be replaced with smaller combat-type numerals. TAC's lightning-strike shield went on the tails and pilots scribed their names beside the cockpits, while 'Flying Eight Ball' and other personalised designs were painted on the fuselages. Later, the mottoes and insignia had to be removed.

The squadrons had to be packed and ready to go on a moment's notice. Obtaining the necessary supplies for the prerequisite flyaway kits wasn't easy, but somehow the supply officers dug them up.

The new units scheduled for deployment had the added responsibility of reactivating bases overseas, including providing billeting, mess facilities, base exchanges, and servicemen's clubs, and get a whole base in operation.

Because the ANG had no aerial refuelling training – or, on some aircraft, not even the capability for it– the planes would have to land-hop across the Atlantic. That meant the F-86Hs and T-33s flew the northern route, through Newfoundland, Greenland, Iceland, and Scotland. The F-84Fs and RF-84Fs flew via Newfoundland, the Azores and Spain. No RF-84Fs had flown the Atlantic before and only a handful of the Guard pilots had flown across *any* ocean, thus they became pioneers.

Aerospace Defense Command's radar network, plus its RC-121 Warning Star radar surveillance aircraft, played a key role in guiding the fighters over the Arctic route. Strategic Air Command tasked plenty of KC-135 tankers to the operation, which were used mostly for communication relay rather than aerial gas stations. Movement control teams (MCT) were stationed at staging bases along the various routes: CFB Goose Bay in Newfoundland, Sondrestrom in Greenland, and Lajes in the Azores. The teams were responsible for preparing for the incoming planes, refuelling them, taking care of the crews, providing maintenance if required, briefing the aircrews and relaunching the planes. Tactical Air Command's C-135 aerial command post, equipped with a suite of radio equipment, also took part in the operation.

The Guard units started their exodus on October 27. The F-84Fs and RF-84Fs moved to McGuire AFB in New Jersey, while the F-86Hs and T-33s went to Loring AFB, Maine. From McGuire, the F-84Fs moved to Harmon in Newfoundland, the RF-84Fs went to the Naval Air Station at Argentia, Newfoundland, and the F-86Hs and T-33s moved to Goose Bay.

Thanks to good weather, the F-86Hs began their crossing two days ahead of schedule, starting the 874nm leg to Sondrestrom on October 30. The T-33s followed on November 1, the same day the F-84Fs and RF-84s began their long flights to the Azores. For both types, the leg to the Azores represented a challenge. The F-84F's route was 1,481nm, a distance that demanded a 15kts tailwind if they were to reach Lajes with a comfortable margin of fuel. The same demands were placed on the RF-84s, which had nearly 1,300nm to fly between Argentia and Lajes, with 400 fewer pounds of fuel than the F-84Fs. Because of the long distance to be flown, the F-84Fs were towed to the end of the Argentia runway for starting. The planes were tilted so that fuel could be packed into the forward sections of the pylon tanks. Under normal refuelling, the tanks didn't get quite filled.

The deployment represented one of the most challenging yet spectacularly successful tests in the ANG's history to date. It only took 27 days for the F-84Fs and RF-84s, F-86Hs and T-33s to get on their way. The three F-104 squadrons, activated on November 1, went through a transition almost as supersonic as their aircraft. Previously assigned to the Aerospace Defense Command, they were reassigned to Tactical Air Command and on their way overseas a scant ten days after activation. The main force of aircraft began leaving their home bases on October 27 and, 12 days later, all 218 were at their new bases overseas. All but six were there in nine days, because they were delayed at Lajes to wait for parts from the US. And the entire deployment was made without a single accident.

After the move, Air Force Secretary Eugene Zuckert commented: "The way the deployment was conducted so soon after recall could only be the result of sustained superior performance. It is my desire that every man know of the pride the whole USAF feels in this accomplishment, which reflects the high standards set and maintained in ANG training."

The first F-104 assigned to the 151st Fighter Interceptor Squadron departed Knoxville aboard a Military Air Transport Service C-124 on November 10, followed by the first F-104 assigned to the 197th FIS based at Phoenix on November 16. The two Starfighters were the first of 40 deployed to Ramstein Air Base in West Germany, where the aircraft were reassembled and test flown, an effort completed on December 18. Both squadrons started a 15-minute air defence alert commitment on December 9. During the first six months of 1962, the F-104s deployed to Ramstein were grounded several times for safety reasons.

Moron Air Base in Spain was a second deployment location for ANG F-104s in support of Stair Step. The first of 20 Starfighters assigned to the 157th FIS based at McEntire ANG Base arrived onboard a C-124 transporter on November 12. All 20 aircraft were reassembled, and test flown and, from November 25, the 157th FIS assumed its alert commitment at Moron. By June 25, 1962, the 157th FIS had flown more than 2,500 hours from Moron when the alert was stood down.

During their eight-month deployments to Ramstein and Moron, all the squadrons sent a detachment to Wheelus Air Base, Libya, to fire GAR-8 air-to-air missiles, the then USAF designation for the AIM-9P Sidewinder. All 60 F-104s returned to their home stations in Knoxville, Phoenix and McEntire in early July 1962.

Cuban Missile Crisis

The ANG played a limited role in the most heated Soviet-American confrontation

Below: **Four F-101B Voodoos assigned to North Dakota ANG's 119th Fighter Interceptor Group fly in formation over the mid-west circa 1977.** US Air National Guard

of the Cold War: the Cuban missile crisis in October and November 1962. Although some ANG units were alerted for a possible recall, none were mobilised. The air defence alert commitment of interceptors in Puerto Rico was expanded from 14 to 24-hours a day. Volunteer aircrews from ANG heavy transport units flew 28 special airlift missions during the crisis. USAF bombers and interceptors were dispersed to ANG installations.

Dominican Republic

US President Lyndon B Johnson dispatched troops to the Dominican Republic on April 28, 1965, to evacuate Americans and protect their property during a civil war. The following month, he announced that there were 14,000 US troops on the island to prevent communists from taking over the government. Volunteers from ANG transport units and Oklahoma's Talking Bird flying command post participated in the operation.

Vietnam

On January 23, 1968, the North Koreans seized the US spy ship USS *Pueblo*. President Lyndon B Johnson ordered a limited reserve mobilisation. Next, the Tet offensive by communist troops in South Vietnam in February 1968 stretched American military resources thinner and Johnson ordered another small mobilisation.

In response to the first presidential order, the ANG activated 9,343 personnel on January 25, 1968. Within 36 hours, approximately 95% of the guardsmen had reported to their units. Those included eight tactical fighter groups, three tactical reconnaissance groups and three wing headquarters. The fighter units, which had been beneficiaries of additional resources under the Combat Beef programme, were rated combat-ready when called into federal service. Primarily because of equipment shortages, the reconnaissance units took about a month to prepare themselves for overseas service. An additional 1,333 guardsmen were called up on May 13, including two tactical fighter groups and a medical evacuation unit. The former, equipped with F-86Hs, were sent to Cannon Air Force Base in New Mexico to train pilots as forward air controllers and combat crewmen. The latter transported military patients in the continental US and the Caribbean.

On May 3, F-100s from Colorado ANG's 120th Tactical Fighter Squadron arrived at Phan Rang Air Base in Vietnam. By June 1, all the 120th's pilots were flying combat missions. Meanwhile, the 174th (Iowa), 188th (New Mexico) and 136th (New York) had all deployed to Vietnam with their F-100s. In addition, 85% of the 355th Tactical Fighter Squadron – on paper a regular air force unit – were guardsmen. The ANG units were quickly and effectively integrated into USAF combat operations. On their return home in April 1969, they had flown 24,124 sorties and performed 38,614 combat hours. Those numbers rose to approximately 30,000 sorties and 50,000 hours if the predominantly ANG 355th was included.

Above: **The last F-51 Mustang in squadron service with the USAF retired from West Virginia ANG's 157th Fighter Group on January 27, 1957.** US Air National Guard

Continued on page 16

F-4 MUD-MOVER AND AIR DEFENDER

An overview of the McDonnell-Douglas F-4 Phantom II in Air National Guard service

TWENTY-SEVEN AIR NATIONAL Guard squadrons operated the F-4 Phantom II. All variants – the F-4C, F-4D, F-4E, F-4G and RF-4C – were flown by tactical fighter and reconnaissance squadrons from 24 US states.

Years after the F-4C's first flight on May 27, 1963, 12 ANG squadrons flew the F-4C variant all-weather, ground-attack version powered by two General Electric J79-GE-15 engines, each rated at 17,000lb of thrust with afterburner, equipped with the APQ-100 radar and armed with four AIM-7 Sparrow missiles mounted in recesses under the fuselage and four AIM-4 Falcon or AIM-9 Sidewinder infrared homing air-to-air missiles on the inboard underwing pylon. Air-to-ground missiles integrated on the aircraft included the AGM-12 Bullpup, AGM-45 Shrike and AGM-65 Maverick.

Active-duty USAF F-4Cs were initially assigned to units of the ANG in 1972. First was the 170th TFS of the 183rd TFG of the Illinois ANG, which began to receive the type in January 1972. F-4Cs ended up serving with seven ANG units in the tactical air-to-ground and air-to-air roles with general-purpose fighter squadrons, along with seven in the air defence role with seven fighter interceptor squadrons and an air defence training squadron.

McDonnell-Douglas improved the original F-4C by developing the F-4D equipped with the APQ-109A radar and improved avionics. The F-4D retained the AIM-7 Sparrow capability, but not the AIM-9 Sidewinder, which was replaced by the AIM-4 Falcon infrared homing missile. Since the variant's first flight in June 1965, 12 ANG squadrons have flown the F-4D variant, four of which transitioned from the F-4C.

In the late 1970s and early 1980s, former active-duty USAF F-4Ds were assigned to the ANG. The first unit to operate the F-4D was the 178th FIS of the 119th FIG of the North Dakota ANG, which received its aircraft in March 1977. F-4Ds served both in the tactical fighter and interceptor roles. The last F-4Ds were withdrawn from the fighter interceptor groups of the ANG in 1992.

McDonnell-Douglas further improved the F-4 design by developing the F-4E, powered by improved J79-GE-17 engines generating 900lb of additional static thrust and equipped with the APQ-120 radar with a smaller cross-section to accommodate a 20mm M61A1 Vulcan cannon housed in the elongated nose. Years after the F-4E's first flight on August 1, 1965, five ANG squadrons transitioned from the F-4D to the F-4E.

According to Joe Baugher's excellent website (www.joebaugher.com): "The F-4G was the designation applied to 116 USAF F-4Es that were converted to the Wild Weasel anti-surface-to-air configuration. The prototype YF-4G made its first flight in December 1975.

"The 20mm M61A1 Vulcan cannon and ammunition drum were removed and replaced by an under-nose fairing that housed forward- and side-looking radar antenna, as well as line replacement units for the APR-38 radar warning and attack system, later replaced with the APR-47.

"An F-4G was fitted with 52 receiving and emitting antennas found all over

Below: **F-4D 64-956 assigned to North Dakota ANG's 119th Fighter Interceptor Group 'The Happy Hooligans' once based at Fargo-Hector Field over Crater Lake, Oregon.** US Air National Guard

the aircraft. The main receivers were housed in front of the chin gondola that replaced the M61 cannon, with others being housed in a pod mounted on top of the fin. Eight of the blade antennas that protrude from the fuselage provided low-band omnidirectional signal reception, with five others being directional and capable of giving the threat bearing on the display in the rear cockpit.

"The F-4G retained a Westinghouse APQ-120 radar as installed in the airframe before conversion from F-4E standard, although a new digital processor was added."

F-4C 63-592 assigned to Hawaii Air National Guard's 154th Group over the Pacific Ocean in Hawaii. US Air National Guard

Above: Crew chiefs assigned to Arkansas ANG's 184th Tactical Fighter Group help aircrew board F-4C 63-629 at Howard Air Force Base, Panama. The aircraft is painted in the Southeast Asia colour scheme and a full colour badge depicting a razorback boar. US Air National Guard

Kinetic weapons employed by the F-4G included the AGM-45 Shrike standard anti-radiation missile and the AGM-78 with a longer range and a larger warhead than the Shrike. Eventually the F-4G employed the AGM-88 high-speed anti-radiation missile (HARM) which superseded most of the former anti-radiation weapons, offering a greatly enhanced kill capability and greater launch versatility.

For self-protection, the F-4G could carry up to four AIM-9 Sidewinder and four AIM-7 Sparrow air-to-air missiles, the latter in the under-fuselage slots, although the left-hand front slot often carried an ALQ-119 or ALQ-141 jammer pod.

On April 12, 1991, the US Department of Defense (DOD) announced that the F-4Gs would all be reassigned to the ANG. The 190th Tactical Reconnaissance Squadron of the Idaho ANG began its conversion from the RF-4C to the F-4G in June 1991. Another RF-4C ANG unit, the 192nd TRS of the Nevada ANG, had been scheduled to convert to the F-4G, but the DOD changed its mind in April 1991 and instead the 192nd transitioned from the RF-4C to the C-130H. Consequently, the 190th TRS was the only ANG unit to operate the F-4G.

In April 1993, while based in Saudi Arabia, the then 190th Fighter Squadron took over responsibility for conducting the SEAD role in support of Operation Southern Watch, the enforcement of a no-fly zone over southern Iraq. The Idaho ANG's F-4Gs were later transferred to Incirlik Air Base in Turkey to support Operation Provide Comfort II. Overall, the squadron completed four deployments to the Gulf, the last of which returned to the US in December 1995.

On April 20, 1996, the last F-4Gs were withdrawn from service by the 190th TRS

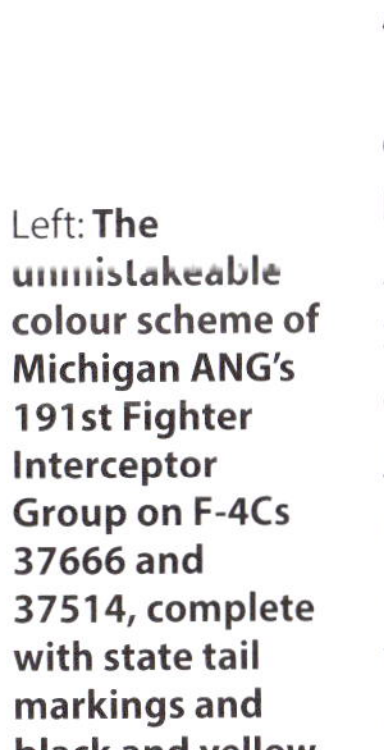

Left: The unmistakeable colour scheme of Michigan ANG's 191st Fighter Interceptor Group on F-4Cs 37666 and 37514, complete with state tail markings and black and yellow checks. Dan Stijovich

Left: F-4D 65648 assigned to Minnesota ANG's 148th Fighter Interceptor Group turns short finals to land at March AFB, California. Dan Stijovich

F-4 PHANTOM II OPERATORS IN THE AIR NATIONAL GUARD

Alabama ANG

116th Tactical Reconnaissance Squadron	117th Tactical Reconnaissance Wing	RF-4C 1971-1994
160th Tactical Reconnaissance Squadron 160th Tactical Fighter Squadron	117th Tactical Reconnaissance Wing 187th Tactical Fighter Group	RF-4C 1971-1983 F-4D 1983-1988

Arkansas ANG

184th Tactical Fighter Squadron	188th Tactical Fighter Group	F-4C 1979-1988

California ANG

194th Fighter Interceptor Squadron	144th Fighter Interceptor Wing	F-4D 1984-1989
196th Tactical Fighter Squadron	163rd Tactical Fighter Group	F-4C 1982-1987 F-4E 1987-1990
196th Tactical Reconnaissance Squadron	163rd Tactical Reconnaissance Group	RF-4C 1990-1993

District of Colombia ANG

121st Tactical Fighter Squadron	113th Tactical Fighter Wing	F-4D 1981-1989

Georgia ANG

128th Tactical Fighter Squadron	116th Tactical Fighter Group	F-4D 1980-1986

Hawaii ANG

199th Tactical Fighter Squadron	154th Group	F-4C 1976-1987

Idaho ANG

190th Tactical Reconnaissance Squadron	124th Tactical Reconnaissance Group	RF-4C 1975-1991
190th Fighter Squadron	124th Fighter Group	F-4G 1991-1996

Illinois ANG

170th Tactical Fighter Squadron	183rd Tactical Fighter Group	F-4C 1972-1981 F-4D 1981-1990

Indiana ANG

163d Tactical Fighter Squadron	122nd Tactical Fighter Group	F-4C 1979-1986 F-4E 1986-1991
113th Tactical Fighter Squadron	181st Tactical Fighter Group	F-4C 1979-1988 F-4E 1988-1991

Kansas ANG

127th and 177th Tactical Fighter Squadrons	184th Tactical Fighter Group	F-4D 1979-1990

Kentucky ANG

165th Tactical Reconnaissance Squadron	123d Tactical Reconnaissance Wing	RF-4C 1976-1988

Louisiana ANG

122d Tactical Fighter Squadron	159th Tactical Fighter Group	F-4C 1979-1986

Michigan ANG

171st Fighter Interceptor Squadron	191st Fighter Interceptor Group	F-4C 1978-1988 F-4D 1988-1991

Minnesota ANG

179th Tactical Reconnaissance Squadron	148th Reconnaissance Group	RF-4C 1976-1983
179th Fighter Interceptor Squadron	148th Fighter Interceptor Group	F-4D 1983-1990

Mississippi ANG

153d Tactical Reconnaissance Squadron	186th Tactical Reconnaissance Group	RF-4C 1978-1991

Missouri ANG

110th Tactical Fighter Squadron	131st Tactical Fighter Group	F-4C 1979-1985 F-4E 1985-1991

Nebraska ANG

173rd Tactical Reconnaissance Squadron	155th Tactical Reconnaissance Group	RF-4C

Nevada ANG

192nd Tactical Reconnaissance Squadron	152nd Tactical Reconnaissance Group	RF-4C 1972-1993

New Jersey ANG

141st Tactical Fighter Squadron	108th Tactical Fighter Group	F-4D 1981-1985 F-4E 1985-1991

New York ANG

136th Fighter-Interceptor Squadron	107th Fighter-Interceptor Group	F-4C 1982-1986 F-4D 1986-1990

North Dakota ANG

178th Fighter-Interceptor Squadron	119th Fighter-Interceptor Group	F-4D 1977-1990

Oregon ANG

123rd Fighter Interceptor Squadron	142nd Fighter Interceptor Group	F-4C 1981-1989
114th Tactical Fighter Training Squadron	142nd Tactical Fighter Wing	F-4C 1983-1989

Texas ANG

111th Fighter Interceptor Squadron	147th Fighter Interceptor Group	F-4C 1982-1987 F-4D 1987-1989
182nd Tactical Fighter Squadron	149th Tactical Fighter Group	F-4C 1979-1986

Vermont ANG

134th Tactical Fighter Squadron	158th Tactical Fighter Group	F-4D 1982-1986

RF-4C 64-077 assigned to Alabama ANG's 117th Reconnaissance Wing landing at its home station at Birmingham International Airport, Alabama, in 1993. Dan Stijovich

F-4E 67-348 of California ANG's 163rd Tactical Fighter Group landing at its home base at March Air Reserve Base, California, in 1989. Dan Stijovich

F-4D 66-649 assigned to Alabama ANG's 187th Tactical Fighter Group at Nellis Air Force Base during Exercise Gunsmoke 1987. Dan Stijovich

and delivered to Davis-Monthan Air Force Base for storage with the Aerospace Maintenance And Regeneration Center. This marked the final departure of the F-4 Phantom from active-duty service with any American unit.

McDonnell-Douglas also developed a tactical reconnaissance variant of the F-4C, designated the RF-4C, which was designed for all-weather operation equipped with the APQ-172 radar (originally the APQ-99). According to the National Museum of the US Air Force, the RF-4C development programme began in 1962 and the first production aircraft made its maiden flight on May 18, 1964. The RF-4C could carry a variety of cameras in three different stations in its nose, with a high and low altitude, day or night capability. A centre line pod housing a high-resolution long range oblique photography camera was an optional system.

Ahead of deployment to the US Central Command's area of responsibility, RF-4Cs assigned to the Alabama and Nevada ANG units were modified to carry AIM-9 Sidewinders.

Right: **RF-4C 65-838 from Nebraska ANG's 155th Tactical Reconnaissance Group landing at Nellis Air Force Base during Exercise Red Flag 1991.** Dan Stijovich

F-4E 68-345 of Missouri ANG's 131st Tactical Fighter Wing landing at Nellis Air Force Base. Dan Stijovich

Below: **F-4G 69-303 assigned to Idaho ANG's 124th Fighter Group trails a drag chute after landing at March AFB, California. The aircraft is loaded with two inert CATM-88 HARM missiles.** Dan Stijovich

Continued from page 11

Two ANG fighter squadrons and their F-100Cs were dispatched to South Korea in the summer of 1968 to replace the USAF units that had been rushed there during the *Pueblo* crisis. The 166th (Ohio) and 127th (Kansas) were formed into the 354th Tactical Fighter Wing. Except for the two flying squadrons, the wing consisted of individual Guard members and Air Force Reservists from other units. Once the *Pueblo*'s crew was returned, the guardsmen returned to the US and left federal service shortly after.

The 123rd TRW experienced a difficult tour of duty. The wing and its four units – the 123rd Tactical Reconnaissance Group (Kentucky), 189th TRG (Arkansas), 152nd TRG (Nevada), and the 123rd Reconnaissance Technical Squadron (Arkansas) – had not been rated combat-ready when mobilised on January 27, 1968, primarily due to equipment shortages. The l23rd's RF-101s began functioning as the primary USAF tactical reconnaissance platforms in the continental US elements of its squadrons and rotated temporary duty assignments in Japan and Korea from July 1968 until April 1969, providing photo reconnaissance support to US forces in those areas.

ANG volunteers also supported air force operations in Southeast Asia. The first sizeable ANG airlift began in 1965, and they flew regularly until 1972. Between August and September 1965, ANG domestic and offshore medical evacuation flights freed active-duty USAF resources for such missions.

In July 1970, two EC-121 Super Constellations from Pennsylvania's 193rd Tactical Electronic Warfare

Above: **KC-97F Stratofreighter 10329 assigned to Georgia ANG's 116th Air Transport Wing based at Dobbins Air Force Base in Marietta. The unit operated the type between 1961 and 1965.** US Air National Guard

Squadron departed their home station for Korat, Thailand. During the next six months, about 60 Guardsmen were rotated through Korat on 30- to 60-day tours for Operation Commando Buzz. Their aircraft served as flying radar stations and airborne control platforms for US air operations until January 1971.

Operation Just Cause

Operation Just Cause was mounted from December 20, 1989, to January 11, 1990, to expel Manuel Noriega, the dictator of Panama, and install the democratically-elected president. ANG units participated in the operation because of their regularly scheduled presence in Panama for Operations Coronet Cove and Volant Oak. Only Pennsylvania's 193d Special Operations Group (SOG) was part of the integral planning process by the Joint Chiefs of Staff and the Air Staff for the invasion of Panama. The 105th Military Airlift Group (MAG) and the 172nd MAG provided airlift support for the operation. They flew 35 missions, completed 138 sorties, moved 1,911 passengers and 1,404.7 tonnes of cargo, which expended 434.6 flying hours. ANG Volant Oak C-130 aircrews flew 22 missions, completed 181 sorties, moved 3,107 passengers and 551.3 tonnes of cargo, which expended 140.1 flying hours. The ANG Coronet Cove units, the 114th TFG and the 180th TFG, flew 34 missions, completed 34 sorties, expended 71.7 flying hours, and expended 2,715 rounds of ordnance.

First Gulf War

On August 2, 1990, Iraq seized its tiny oil-rich neighbour Kuwait. US President George Bush rushed American military forces to the region and assembled a broad

Right: **RF-84F Thunderstreak 11879 assigned to Iowa ANG's 185th Tactical Fighter Group parked on the ramp at Sioux City Airport.** US Air National Guard

Right: **F-84F Thunderstreak 11747 assigned to Ohio ANG's 178th Tactical Fighter Group on a mission over Alaska during Operation Punchcard IV in November 1968.** US Air National Guard

Left: **Georgia ANG's 116th Air Transport Wing based at Dobbins Air Force Base in Marietta transitioned from the KC-97F Stratofreighter to the C-124C Globemaster II in 1965.** US Air National Guard

international coalition against the Iraqis. Altogether, 12,404 guardsmen entered federal service during Operations Desert Shield and Desert Storm. Of that number, 5,240 deployed to Southwest Asia, while another 6,264 served in the continental US. The remaining 900 were assigned to Europe and other overseas locations.

Initially, Guard volunteers concentrated on airlifting, as well as flying air refuelling, reconnaissance, tactical airlift, and special operations missions. More than 8,000 guardsmen entered active duty as volunteers during Desert Shield and Desert Storm. Altogether, 10,456 guardsmen were mobilised for active duty during the First Gulf War, including 1,160 in fighter and reconnaissance units. It was the first time in the ANG's history that most mobilised personnel had not been members of combat flying units. Instead, they were members of mission support units.

Unlike most previous mobilisations, ANG units had not required additional training or new equipment. Although the ANG in effect had to reinvent itself through an unprecedented level of volunteerism and tailored packages as Desert Shield unfolded, its units entered federal service and were rapidly deployed where needed. ANG RF-4C aircraft flew 1,045 tactical reconnaissance missions, including 350 in combat. ANG fighters participated in the air campaign from the first day.

By the time the war ended, its F-16s had flown 3,645 missions and dropped 3,500 tonnes of ordnance without losing a single aircraft to enemy fire. In the special operations arena, Pennsylvania ANG EC-130s had flown approximately 2,000 missions lasting some 8,000 hours. They broadcast surrender appeals and instructions to Iraqi soldiers.

The ANG's largest contributions – as gauged by the numbers of personnel involved – were concentrated in a wide range of support missions. The Guard's aerial tankers pumped more than 250 million pounds of fuel into more than 18,000 aircraft. Its airlifters flew some 40,000 hours, transporting 55,000 people and 115,000 tonnes of cargo.

After the Storm

After Operation Desert Storm in 1991, the ANG continued to adjust to the realities of the post-Cold War era and began to posture itself for the 21st Century.

Below: **F-100D Super Sabre fighters assigned to Connecticut ANG's 103rd Tactical Fighter Group in formation during a mission flown from Bradley Field in Windsor Locks, Connecticut in 1975.** US Air National Guard

That meant coping with a higher operations tempo using packages of volunteers to augment the active force in a series of contingency and humanitarian relief operations overseas, a continued shift from a predominant fighter force to a more balanced one that included both fighters and a significant increase in the numbers of larger aircraft.

The ANG completed the process of taking over 1st Air Force from the active force with its air defence and air sovereignty missions on October 1, 1997. It also gained a toehold in space missions after years of effort and assumed total responsibility for airlift support of the National Science Foundation in Antarctica from the US Navy. In addition, it reorganised its headquarters within the National Guard Bureau and the ANG Readiness Center and launched an ambitious staff integration programme with the active force.

At the end of 1997, the ANG had 110,025 assigned military personnel. That represented a modest decrease from its 1994 end strength of 113,587. Of those, 33,422 – comprising 22,862 civil service technicians and 10,560 Active Guard/ Reserve (AGR) members – were full-time support personnel as of September 30, 1997. Those numbers represented a slight increase from the 32,616 full-time personnel – 23,304 technicians and 9,312 AGRs – at the end of 1994. Technicians were federal civil servants administered by the states who were also military members of their Guard units; AGRs were full-time military members of their units.

Most of the ANG's personnel, funds and equipment was concentrated in its flying units. They operated primarily from civilian airports and other installations outside active-duty military bases, as they had since the end of World War Two. The ANG's equipment inventory included 1,162 primary assigned aircraft (PAA) as of September 30, 1997, a significant reduction from the 1,505 PAA in its inventory six years earlier. During that period, the composition of the ANG's inventory had changed significantly. Following a trend that had begun in 1955, when the ANG had acquired its first four airlift units, it had evolved from a predominantly fighter-attack-reconnaissance (FAR) force to one whose units were almost evenly balanced between FAR and large aircraft such as airlifters, tankers, and heavy bombers. The ANG's fighter wing equivalents (FWE) were reduced in 1995 from 8.5 to 6, consistent with the Defense Guidance that sized the total USAF at 20 FWE (13 active duty, six ANG and one Air Force Reserve). Heavy bombers entered the ANG's inventory for the first time in 1994, with 14 B-1Bs programmed by the end of 1997 for two units, the 184th Bomb Wing (BW), Kansas, and the 116th BW, Georgia.

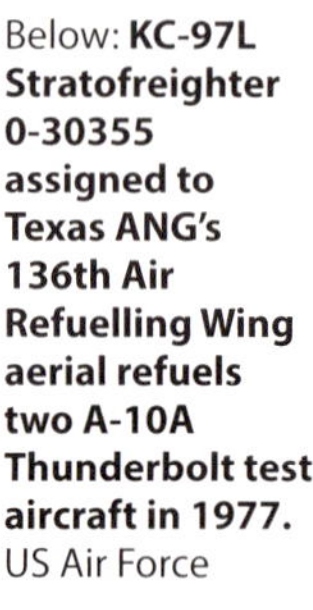

Below: **KC-97L Stratofreighter 0-30355 assigned to Texas ANG's 136th Air Refuelling Wing aerial refuels two A-10A Thunderbolt test aircraft in 1977.** US Air Force

In the early 1990s, the ANG's senior Pentagon leadership had begun reshaping the reserve component for the post-Cold War era. Following a series of give-and-take discussions between senior USAF leaders, ANG long range planners and the individual states, a strategic vision for the future was unveiled during the fall of 1992. Major Generals Philip Killey [ANG Director, November 1988 to January 1994] and Donald Shepperd [ANG Director, January 1994 to January 1998] stressed that the ANG could not avoid the far-reaching changes sweeping through the US armed forces. While downsizing active force flying units, the USAF wanted to retain all ANG and Air Force Reserve units as a cost-effective way to maintain force structure.

Nevertheless, the ANG's core fighter force was bound to shrink dramatically as the USAF reduced to 22 or fewer tactical FWEs. To preserve its flying units, the ANG would aggressively seek alternative missions for some, reduce their number of assigned aircraft, combine units at the same location and, as a last resort, close units. Airlifters, tankers, and bombers appeared to offer some opportunities for growth in the ANG. Furthermore, the senior leadership would aggressively seek out new missions for some of the ANG's non-flying units. They predicted that the

Guard's assigned personnel strength, which was approximately 118,000 in 1992, would shrink significantly, although they doubted that it would go below 100,000 even in a worst-case scenario. During the restructuring, it was essential that the ANG maintain a high level of readiness. It was also stressed that the ANG accomplish the changes in a co operative manner with the USAF. The ANG depended on a healthy air force and could not afford to get into a fight over diminishing post-Cold War defence resources.

The ANG's continued ability to provide properly equipped units also depended heavily on equipment modernisation. Although it normally relied on the fall-out from the active force, government support played an important role. Due to lobbying by the Mississippi congressional delegation, the USAF announced that it would equip the 172nd AW with C-17s. Original plans to equip two ANG squadrons with C-17s had been dropped when aircraft procurement was cut back drastically in the early 1990s. Through a separately-funded Guard and Reserve Equipment Account (GREA) established by the US Congress in 1982, significant numbers of new C-130s had been purchased for the ANG in recent years. With its airlift fleet increasingly called upon to operate in dangerous areas

around the world, the ANG supported USAF efforts to equip those aircraft with defensive systems.

Congressional initiatives had also enabled the ANG to complete the replacement of 1950s vintage C-130B models with modern C-130H aircraft. The ANG and USAF were also working closely to develop unit training devices for F-15 and F-16 units. That low-cost device relied on off-the-shelf equipment that replaced existing simulators that were 20 to 30 times more expensive. For night operations, the ANG was working with ACC to test low cost, off-the-shelf equipment that would allow its A-10s, F-15s, and F-16s to be more effective night-fighters. The first step was to upgrade its A-10 fleet.

In 1995, Massachusetts ANG's 104th Fighter Wing became the first ANG unit to use night vision goggles in combat. During March 1995, the ANG also began to develop a manned tactical reconnaissance capability to replace the RF-4Cs that were being retired from its aircraft inventory. The 192nd Fighter Wing in Virginia developed the concept and established an initial operational capability with four F-16s, four reconnaissance pods and 12 trained pilots. The new equipment, based upon modern digital technology, replaced older, manpower-intensive, wet film technology.

Above: **F-105G Thunderchief 62-347 from Kansa ANG's 184th Tactical Fighter Training Group. The group operated the type between 1971-1979.** US Air Force

Continued on page 24

AIR GUARD
SLUFS

The Ling-Temco-Vought A-7D Corsair II in Air National Guard service

IN 1973, NEW Mexico Air National Guard's 150th Tactical Fighter Group became the first ANG squadron to receive the A-7D Corsair. Colorado and Ohio ANG wings began receiving former active-duty A-7Ds in 1974, followed by South Carolina and Puerto Rico in 1975. Further A-7Ds were transferred to Iowa and South Dakota in 1976, followed by Arizona and Michigan in 1978. The last ANG squadrons equipped with the A-7D were the Pennsylvania unit in 1980 and Oklahoma and Virginia in 1981.

Notable Events

New Mexico's 150th TFG was the first ANG unit to be assigned to the Rapid Deployment Joint Task Force, the first to participate in Exercise Bright Star in Egypt, the first to receive the Low Altitude Night Attack modification to the A-7 and the first to complete a deployed bare base operational readiness inspection, all in 1980. The unit also set an A-7D endurance record of 11.5 hours for a non-stop flight from Pease Air Force Base, New Hampshire, to Cairo West Air Base, Egypt, for Bright Star.

Colorado ANG's 140th TFG received its first A-7D in 1974, followed by brand-new Corsairs procured in FY1975 and FY1976. Congress approved the purchase to keep the LTV production line in Dallas open and the workers employed in the wake of post-Vietnam Department

of Defense reductions. The group received brand-new twin-seat A-7Ks trainers in 1983.

Colorado deployed all 24 of its assigned A-7s to Merzifon Air Base, Turkey during September and October 1979 for 30 days under Exercise Coronet Rider. The event was the first time any ANG unit had deployed to a location under bare base conditions.

The Ohio ANG was the largest operator of the A-7D with three tactical fighter groups assigned the LTV attack aircraft. The 121st TFW began conversion to the A-7D in December 1974, the 178th TFG in January 1978 and the 180th TFG in the summer of 1979. The 178th's conversion from the F-100 to the A-7 was accomplished in less than three months, the fastest ever for a USAF or ANG unit.

Ohio ANG's three A-7 units completed three deployments to RAF Sculthorpe in England in 1983 for Coronet Castle (24), 1986 for Coronet Miami (24) and 1989 for Coronet Pine (18).

In 1989, while deployed to Panama for a Coronet Cove exercise, A-7Ds assigned to the 180th TFG were employed during Operation Just Cause.

Puerto Rico ANG's 156th TFG used the A-7D's capabilities to define mission success in the air-defence role surrounding the Caribbean island and during frequent deployments to the Panama Canal Zone. Because of its endurance, the A-7 could fly directly from Puerto Rico to Panama.

In 1977, Arizona ANG's 162nd Tactical Fighter Training Group retired its F-100 Super Sabres and received A-7Ds for assignment to the resident 152nd Tactical Fighter Training Squadron. The 162nd TFTG received the two-seat A-7K in 1981 and 1982: the A-7K was designed specifically to meet the ANG's A-7 pilot training programme. Two additional squadrons were assigned to the 162nd TFTG to meet the pilot training demand: the 195th TFTS in February 1984 and the 148th TFTS in October 1985.

During 1985, the 162nd TFTG also started F-16 pilot training.

Virginia ANG's 192nd TFG started converting to the A-7D in October 1981. Six months later, the unit was declared operationally ready, and, in June 1982, it was decreed combat ready by a 9th Air Force team when the unit passed a deployed operational readiness inspection at Travis ANG Base, Savannah, Georgia. In September 1985, the group deployed to Evenes Air Station, Norway, 150 miles above the Arctic Circle, for Coronet Panther.

Coronet Buffalo

Up until 1963, NATO's defence policy was 'Mutually Assured Destruction', which relied on the deterrent effect of nuclear weapons. It was decided at a NATO summit that year to change to what was called 'Flexible Response', where aggression from the USSR would be met by a conventional reply, using nuclear weapons only as a final option.

Above: **New Mexico Air National Guard's 150th Tactical Fighter Group became the first ANG squadron to receive A-7D Corsairs in 1973.** US Air National Guard

This placed more responsibility on non-nuclear forces to hold the line. If tensions had increased to the brink of war, large numbers of American aircraft would have flown into Europe to counter the numerically superior Warsaw Pact forces. These aircraft would have been stationed at US bases and those of other NATO members. Such locations were referred to as co-located operating

A-7D CORSAIR FACTS

The A-7D Corsair was powered by an Allison TF41-A-1 turbofan engine rated at 14,500lb of thrust. It was equipped with an APQ-126 radar and armed with a single 20mm M61A-1 Vulcan six-barrel cannon with 1,000 rounds. For self-defence it could carry AIM-9P Sidewinder air-to-air missiles. The A-7 could carry up to 15,000lb of munitions, 500lb and 1,000lb dumb bombs and AGM-65 Maverick air-to-ground missiles on eight hardpoints to attack armour.

The first A-7D made its maiden flight on September 26, 1968. A combat-capable, two-seat version of the Corsair II was produced for the USAF as the A-7K. The aircraft's second cockpit was possible through the removal of a fuel tank housed in the fuselage. A-7Ks provided a training capability to the six ANG units that operated it. There was one A-7D converted to A-7K configuration, followed by 31 new-build aircraft for the ANG.

The A-7 was a capable fighter aircraft, but more tailored to air-to-ground bombing and area defence missions as it had an incredible fuel load and loiter time, even when flown at heavy weights. The jets could perform aerial refuelling and used this capability to extend their missions and ability to deploy.

The front and rear of the A-7 has a clipped appearance, and the aircraft was often referred to as the 'SLUF' or 'Short Little Ugly Fellow'.

bases. Squadrons were assigned to a specific base and deployed there to become familiar with and train from their wartime station.

Exercise Coronet Buffalo involved the deployment of 36 A-7D aircraft assigned to South Dakota ANG's 114th TFG and Iowa ANG's 132nd and 185th TFGs. All 36 primary aircraft arrived at RAF Waddington, Lincolnshire, England, on May 11, 1985, with tanker support and without the need to call upon the air spares.

Flying operations involved the A-7s conducting simulated wartime missions into mainland Europe and then recovering back to Lincolnshire. This involved striking air defence sites, providing close air support for troops in contact and interdiction hitting fuel refineries, manufacturing sites and lines of communications behind enemy lines.

The three units flew groups of aircraft to Leeuwarden Air Base, the Netherlands and Wittmund Air Base, Germany for 48-hour detachments to fly against resident F-16s and F-4s, respectively. In the UK, the units dropped practice

Above: **A-7D 74-742/PT assigned to Pennsylvania's 112th Tactical Fighter Group in the European One colour scheme.** US Air National Guard

bombs on Wainfleet and Holbeach ranges in Lincolnshire.

ANG pilots rated the aircraft as one of the most accurate bombers the USAF had prior to precision-guided munitions, and they were highly capable at low-level given their upgraded navigation with a projected map display that was aligned with the inertial navigation system [INS].

Coronet Buffalo provided an opportunity for pilots assigned to all three units to interact and deploy together and fly each other's aircraft and for the maintenance personnel to work with each other.

A-7K 81-0077/IA assigned to the 132nd Tactical Fighter Group in a two-tone grey colour scheme in 1989. US Air National Guard

Continued from page 19

Left: **F-15A Eagles from Massachusetts ANG's 102nd Fighter Wing based at Otis Air National Guard Base on combat air patrol during Operation Noble Eagle.** US Air National Guard

As early as February 1988, ANG senior leaders and long-range planners had begun discussing ways to involve the ANG in military space missions. The 1990 ANG Long Range Plan urged the ANG to actively pursue support and operational roles in space. That interest was sparked by a determination to diversify the ANG's fighter-oriented force structure and gain a foothold in emerging missions in the waning years of the Cold War. Senior leaders and planners were convinced that guardsmen could bring valuable skills to the space mission, but it would be very difficult to convince the active force that space provided appropriate opportunities for the ANG. That proved to be an understatement.

The ANG identified 11 possible space missions for further review in October 1991 and detailed concept papers were put together for each of them. But initial discussions with Air Staff and Air Force Space Command (AFSPC) went nowhere. Congress set the stage for progress in the 1993 DOD Appropriations Report, when it directed the ANG to establish a Command, Control, Communications, and Intelligence (C3I) planning office by January 1, 1993, headed by a colonel to investigate potential ANG missions in those areas including space. Consequently, the ANG established a three-person C3I Long Range Planning Office (LRPO) within the NGB in January 1993. That office was placed administratively under the Air Directorate's Operations, Plans and

Programs organisation in October 1993. The ANG also added an advisor to the Air Force Space Command (AFSPC) staff in early 1993 to handle space issues.

The ANG launched an initiative to educate as many USAF space specialists as possible about the ANG and its potential. The ANG was prepared to provide some personnel offsets, but the air force would have to transfer the operations and maintenance funding. The ANG was especially interested in three missions. The first was a mobile command and control system which served as the Commander In Chief's 'looking glass' in the event of a nuclear crisis in the absence of an aircraft. It was a mobility mission that required a big staff and lots of money to maintain during a war but was hardly ever deployed in peacetime. The second was a space warning squadron at Holloman Air Force Base, New Mexico, which had a survival and missile warning mission in the event of a nuclear attack. The third involved operating two Pave Paws ballistic missile early warning radar sites.

On June 30, 1995, the USAF publicly announced structural changes that resulted in the creation of the ANG's first space unit (devoted to the space warning mission). The 138th Air Control Squadron and the 154th Air Control Group, Colorado ANG, were going to be inactivated later in the year, which would affect almost 280 people. The 4th Space Warning Squadron's mission would transfer from the USAF to the ANG and

its basic mission would be to keep the national command authority informed of missile activity worldwide in the event of a nuclear war or other crisis.

The new unit was activated as the 137th Space Warning Squadron, Colorado ANG, on January 21, 1996, at Greeley, Colorado, after gaining federal recognition on October 1, 1995. It consisted of six separate flights to be

Below: **A C-141B Starlifter from Tennessee ANG's 164th Airlift Wing on the ramp at Naval Air Station Sigonella, Italy, in support of Operation Enduring Freedom.** US Air National Guard

manned 45% by full-timers, primarily because of the intense maintenance on its equipment. By the end of 1997, approximately 60% of the unit consisted of full-timers due to the high operations tempo associated with around-the-clock operations.

Maintaining the air defence and air sovereignty of the CONUS were federal missions accomplished by 1st Air Force, a numbered air force (NAF) assigned to the ACC. In 1994, the ANG had begun taking over 1st Air Force, which provided the command-and-control mechanisms for the air defence and air sovereignty of the continental United States. The original conversations proposing that transition had taken place between Major General Killey, then ANG Director, and General Robert Russ, then Tactical Air Command Commander, during 1990-1991. General Russ, a strong supporter of the ANG, had originated the dialogue. He had noted that all the fighter interceptor squadrons defending the CONUS by that time were ANG units, because defence of the homeland had seemed a natural fit. The USAF had wanted to transfer responsibility for resourcing that mission to the ANG primarily for two reasons. First, it needed to reduce its own end strength because of post-Cold War downsizing. Second, it thought the ANG was in a better position to politically defend that mission, which had been coming under increasing attack as expensive and unnecessary.

For their part, ANG senior leaders wanted to maintain as much of its fighter interceptor force structure as possible. Moreover, they needed to find new missions for much of its combat communications and tactical air control units, which faced dramatic drawdowns in the early 1990s. The BRAC report of March 1993 gave the transfer proposal additional impetus. It directed the USAF to either move the Northeast Air Defense Sector (NEADS) from Griffiss Air Force Base, New York, or give it to the ANG. Since ACC did not want to move it and was unable to consolidate it with another sector, transfer to the ANG appeared to be a logical choice. Following discussions between General Killey and senior USAF leadership, agreement was reached to transfer the entire responsibility for 1st Air Force to the ANG. In September 1993, Secretary of Defense Les Aspin approved the changeover.

On January 28, 1994, General Killey, who had just stepped down as ANG Director, assumed command of 1st Air Force as directed by General Merrill McPeak, the Chief of Staff for the air force. With that action, the main impetus for completing the transition to ANG control shifted to Tyndall Air Force Base in Florida from the NGB, the Air Staff, NORAD and Headquarters, ACC. However, the transfer was also intended to place the Chief of the NGB and the ANG Director in partnership with the Commander, 1st Air Force to assist the transition. Throughout the conversion process, all affected units had to maintain combat-ready status.

On December 1, 1994, Headquarters NEADS was redesignated Headquarters Northeast Air Defense Sector (ANG). During 1995, USAF leadership directed the acceleration of the transfer process and won approval from the Office of the Assistant Secretary of Defense for Reserve Affairs to hire an additional 182 AGR personnel to help accomplish it. In October 1995, the Southeast Air Defense Squadron and the Western Air Defense Squadron were constituted and allotted to the NGB.

Command relationships for the 1st Air Force were relatively complicated by traditional ANG standards. The NAF came under ACC, which as the force provider to NORAD was responsible for providing organised, trained, and equipped units that maintained air

Below: **The ramp at Wheeler Sack Army Airfield, Fort Drum, New York, during the Hawgsmoke 2002 competition, showing 58 A-10 attack aircraft, many assigned to ANG wings.** US Air National Guard

defence and air sovereignty for the Continental United States NORAD Region (CONAR). The NGB was responsible for ensuring that 1st Air Force was properly resourced, particularly its operations and maintenance as well as its military personnel budgets. ACC remained responsible for major systems acquisition, including modernisation of the NAF's sector and regional operations centres. NORAD continued as the war-fighting command that 1st Air Force was responsible to in the execution of its operational missions.

All of this was further complicated by the fact that most 1st Air Force personnel were Guardsmen who remained in state status (Title 32, US Code) while organising, training, and equipping for their federal missions. They automatically converted to federal status (Title 10, US Code) when conducting missions such as intercepts of unidentified aircraft entering US airspace because air defence and sovereignty remained federal, not ANG, missions. Likewise, certain officers such as the ROC/SOC commanders always remained in Title 10 status to insure an unbroken federal chain of command.

The size and composition of 1st Air Force's flying unit force structure continued to be a major issue during the transition. Over the decades, the air defence interceptor force defending North America had been dramatically reduced from a high of 2,600 dedicated aircraft (including the Royal Canadian Air Force) in 1958. By February 1996, it had shrunk to 20 ANG fighters at 10 alert locations for CONAR. However, 1st Air Force continued to face strong budgetary pressure to either eliminate or dramatically reduce dedicated ANG fighter interceptor units for air defence and air sovereignty.

The Office of the Secretary of Defense rejected efforts to include language in the 1996 and 1997 Defense Program Guidance to include air sovereignty and air defence as a stated mission and organise resources for them. In 1996, the General Accounting Office (GAO) criticised the ANG for continuing to maintain 150 fighters in 10 dedicated units to defend the US against invading enemy bombers, at a cost of nearly $500 million annually, nearly half-a-decade after the Soviet Union's demise. The GAO urged that the ten ANG units be either disbanded or given other missions. That criticism was well established in Washington, DC. General Colin Powell, while chairman of the JCS, had advocated an end to dedicated continental air defence force in 1993, as had the GAO a year later. Both suggested that general-purpose fighter forces of the air force, navy, and Marines – both active duty and reserve components – could accomplish the mission.

By the end of 1997, the ANG had assumed total responsibility the 1st Air Force, including its three Regional Operational Control Centers and its Sector Operations Control Center, as well as its NAF headquarters. The transition to the ANG was officially complete, representing a major change in the ANG's historic role, executing the command-and-control function for a full-time USAF mission.

But 1st Air Force faced a difficult balancing act and an uncertain future. Continuing pressure to balance the federal budget and the absence of an international peer competitor suggested that its very survival, especially its dedicated fighter-interceptor force, would remain an issue. General Killey turned over responsibility for dealing with such questions when he relinquished command of 1st Air Force to Brigadier General Larry Arnold upon his retirement from active duty at Tyndall Air Force Base, Florida, effective December 18, 1997.

In addition to space and the 1st Air Force, another mission which the ANG agreed to take on was providing airlift support for the National Science Foundation's (NSF) activities in Antarctica. In early 1996, it was announced that the 109th Airlift Wing at Stratton ANG Base in Scotia, New York,

Below: **F-16C 86-364/OH assigned to Ohio ANG's 178th Fighter Wing once based at Springfield-Beckley Airport, Ohio, on a mission from the Combat Regional Training Center at Savannah Air National Guard Base, Georgia.** US Air National Guard

would assume that entire mission from the US Navy in 1999. The 109th, which operated ski-equipped LC-130s, had been flying some NSF support missions to Antarctica since 1988, having flown scientific and military missions to Greenland and the Arctic since 1975. The Antarctic operation would be fully funded by the NSF and the 109th expected to add approximately 235 full-time personnel to support it.

The possibility of the ANG taking over the Antarctica mission had first emerged in 1988. The 109th had been notified that, almost overnight, one of the Distant Early Warning (DEW) Line radar sites that it supported in Greenland was going to be shut down. The other sites would soon follow and the 109th would be largely out of business. The unit had been informally keeping tabs on US Navy LC-130 operations supporting the NSF in Antarctica. Because its aircraft were older than the ANG's and several of them were entering an extensive period of depot maintenance, the US Navy asked if the 109th could provide a limited emergency search and rescue (SAR) capability for two years. The ANG accepted. At that time, it had no thought of taking over the mission entirely. The 109th believed that it was senseless for its aircraft to deploy to the Antarctic and just wait to conduct emergency SAR missions, so it asked the US Navy if it could help carry cargo to the South Pole. The Navy resisted at first, because its procedures and cargo

configurations differed from those of the ANG, but eventually it relented. The main mission of the US Navy and ANG C-130s was to airlift fuel and supplies to the NSF's South Pole Station so that its personnel could survive in isolation during the long Antarctic winter from February to October.

An ANG working group was formed to study the idea in 1990. The following year, a dialogue between the ANG, the Air Staff and the US Navy began. Among other issues, it was difficult at first for the ANG to convince the Air Staff to commit long term resources to an area of the world that had not been declared a warfighting region because of international treaties. The ANG had supported military operations in Greenland and the Arctic (including classified US Navy operations) since the mid-1970s with the ski-equipped C-130s of the 109th AW. It convinced Headquarters, US Air Force that it was not in the nation's best interest to abandon the capability to achieve quick and reliable air access to both polar regions. In March 1993, the US Navy hosted a two-day workshop with representatives of the NSF, ANG, and other interested parties to explore logistics support options for the operation. A draft concept had been prepared by the Air Directorate of the NGB in 1993. In February 1996, a commitment was made to transfer the mission, known as Operation Deep Freeze, and all LC-130

aircraft operated within the DOD to the ANG. In September 1996, senior officers from the 109th AW briefed the NGB on their concept of operations and the status of their preparations to implement Deep Freeze.

Under the transition plan, the ANG would continue to augment the US Navy during the October 1996-March 1997 operating season for the US Antarctic Program. At the end of the October 1997-March 1998 season, the ANG would assume command of the programme. During the third year of the transition in October 1998 to March 1999, the US Navy would augment the ANG before the latter took over the entire programme the following year. There would be seven LC-130s in theatre and they would stage from Christchurch, New Zealand, to McMurdo Station, Antarctica. Traditional Guardsmen, technicians, and the cadre of AGRs specifically brought on board to support Operation Deep Freeze would all be involved in the mission. When fully transitioned to the ANG, the 109th would have ten LC-130s in its inventory. These would include upgrades of the four LC-130 aircraft already in service with the unit, plus three new aircraft and three that would be transferred from the US Navy. ANG estimates of the savings to be realised by consolidating the operation in the hands of the 109th AW ranged from $5 million to $15 million per year. The actual transition to ANG control began in March 1996.

Continued on page 29

AIR CONTROL AND AIR SUPPORT

The Cessna OA-37B Dragonfly in Air National Guard service

THE A-37 DRAGONFLY was developed in 1963 by modifying the Cessna T-37 trainer. It is powered by two General Electric J85-GE-17A turbojet engines, each rated at 2,850lb of thrust. Gutsy by nature, the A-37B was an attack aircraft that carried a 7.62mm minigun mounted in the nose, capable of firing at a rate of 6,000 rounds per minute. Eight hardpoints, four under each wing and each with capacity to carry 1,200lb of ordnance, a machine gun or 2.75-inch rocket pods completed its firepower arsenal and drop tanks.

Vietnam was the type's proving ground and resulted in a refuelling probe being fitted in the nose, along with reticulated foam added to the self-sealing fuel tanks for protection against fire or explosions if hit by anti-aircraft rounds. The cockpit had armour plating fitted and the undercarriage was strengthened to carry increased weight and enable the aircraft to operate from rough remote airstrips. Manoeuvrability, acceleration, rapid deceleration and accurate weapon delivery were all favourable to the pilots who operated the aircraft.

After Vietnam, A-37Bs were transferred from Tactical Air Command to ANG and USAF reserve units and assigned the forward air control role, which was also reflected by its new OA-37B designation, with 'O' denoting observation. Six Tactical Air Support Groups in the Illinois

Right: **OA-37B Dragonfly 73-066/IL assigned to Illinois ANG's 182nd Tactical Air Support Group in 1984. It is painted in the Southeast Asia colour scheme, as applied to the aircraft in Vietnam, and loaded with two drop tanks and a single rocket pod.** US Air National Guard

Right: **A guardsman assigned to Wisconsin ANG's 128th Tactical Air Support Group unloads smoke rockets from a truck and places them in rocket pods ready for loading on an OA-37B Dragonfly.** US Air National Guard

(182nd TASG), Maryland (175th TFW), Michigan, New York (174th TFW), Pennsylvania (111th TASG) and Wisconsin (128th TASG) ANGs operated the OA-37B Dragonfly between 1970 and 1992.

Maryland and New York transitioned to the OA-37B in 1970, followed by Illinois and Wisconsin in 1979 and Pennsylvania and Michigan in 1981. Maryland ANG's 104th Tactical Fighter Squadron trained active-duty USAF special forces personnel in forward air control from Cannon Air Force Base, New Mexico, flying the F-86H Sabre. Its presence in New Mexico was a consequence of the 175th Tactical Fighter Group being federalised and ordered to active service on May 13, 1968. Two year later, the 175th Tactical Fighter Group traded in its F-86H Sabres and received A-37Bs, with which it took up the mission to train to support air force and army special forces.

In March 1970, New York ANG's 174th Tactical Fighter Group also received A-37B, the unit's first aircraft capable of aerial refuelling. This meant the unit was able to conduct training exercises such as Bright Shield in May 1974 and Red Flag in April 1978.

Tail view of an OA-37 Dragonfly as the pilot climbs aboard. The aircraft is assigned to Wisconsin ANG's 128th Tactical Air Support Group. US Air National Guard

Continued from page 27

A chronology of ANG achievements since 1996

December 10, 1996
The last brand-new C-130Hs purchased for the ANG were delivered to Minnesota ANG's 133rd Airlift Wing at Minneapolis International Airport.

July 1997
The USAF halted plans to cut the primary authorised aircraft of five ANG C-130 units from 12 to 8 each.

October 1, 1997
The Continental United States NORAD Region (CONR) and the 1st Air Force officially completed transition to manning by the ANG, replacing active-duty air force personnel.

November 18, 1997
The ANG's Northeast Tanker Task Force (TTF) at Bangor ANGB, Maine, began around-the-clock operations for Operation Phoenix Scorpion, in response to Saddam Hussein's refusal to allow UN experts to inspect dozens of facilities suspected of hiding chemical and biological weapons in Iraq. The TTF, comprising four active-duty and ten ANG KC-135s, pumped over 1 million pounds of jet fuel into USAF aircraft during the week-long operation.

August 4, 1998
The USAF unveiled plans to reorganise more than 2,000 aircraft into ten air expeditionary forces (AEFs) to ease the strain of increased post-Cold War operations overseas. The AEFs would draw upon ANG, Air Force Reserve, and active-duty assets.

December 1998
Six ANG fighter units were unable to enforce the no-fly zones over Iraq because their F-16s lacked the precision-guided munitions and targeting pods that were now required to operate in that region. ANG officials reported they had already begun moving to upgrade F-16s in many states with kits that would enable them to fly night missions and fire precision-guided munitions.

February 1999
ANG KC-135 tankers began providing air refuelling support for fighter movements to Europe and air cargo missions positioning people and supplies for a possible war with the Federal Republic of Yugoslavia over its actions in Kosovo.

March 24, 1999
NATO aircraft began a bombing campaign against Yugoslavia designed to force the Serbs to accept an alliance-sponsored peace agreement for the breakaway province of Kosovo. KC-135 Stratotankers and crews from Hawaii ANG's 203rd Air Refuelling Squadron, on a previously scheduled deployment to France, participated in Operation Allied Force.

March 27, 1999
About 100 ANG volunteers and two EC-130 Commando Solo aircraft from Pennsylvania ANG's 193rd Special Operations Wing deployed to Germany to support the NATO air campaign against Yugoslavia.

April 1, 1999
An EC-130 Commando Solo aircraft assigned to the 193rd Special Operations Wing, Pennsylvania ANG began broadcasting radio and television programmes to northern Serbia as part of Operation Allied Force.

Above: F-102A Delta Dagger 0-41392 of the 119th Fighter Wing, North Dakota ANG, at Hector International Field, North Dakota. US Air Force

Below: A-10C 78-658/PA from the 111th Fighter Wing, Pennsylvania ANG, takes off for a training exercise at Fort Drum, New York armed with an AIM-9 Sidewinder missile, Mk82 500lb practice bombs, an AGM-65 Maverick missile and rocket pods. US Air National Guard

Above: **F-106A Delta Dart 90136 from California ANG's 144th Fighter Interceptor Wing lands at Fresno Air National Guard Base.** US Air National Guard

April 27, 1999
US Secretary of Defense William Cohen announced that President Bill Clinton had approved a Presidential Selective Reserve Call-Up to support the NATO air war for Kosovo, Operation Allied Force. It authorised the mobilisation of up to 33,102 members of the selected reserve. The initial increment of approximately 2,000 would be members of ANG and Air Force Reserve air-refuelling units.

May 1, 1999
Pennsylvania ANG's 171st Air Refuelling Wing (ARW) received its official activation order for Operation Allied Force. The order involved deploying about 400 personnel and 14 KC-135Es to the theatre of operations. Other mobilised ANG tanker units included the 117th ARW from Alabama, 128th ARW from Wisconsin, 141st ARW from Washington, 151st ARW from Utah and the 161st ARW from Arizona.

May 17, 1999
Eighteen ANG A-10s and approximately 510 personnel from the 104th FW, 110th FW and 124th FW left Barnes Municipal Airport, Massachusetts, heading for Italy to participate in Operation Allied Force. They comprised the 104th Expeditionary Operations Group. The 18 aircraft arrived at Trapani Air Base in Sicily two days later and commenced operations on May 21, 1999.

Right: **C-130H transport aircraft from various ANG wings taxi out during Exercise Sentry Cowboy I at Gulfport-Biloxi Airport.** US Air National Guard

May 21, 1999
The acting secretary of the Air Force, F Whitten Peters, directed the mobilisation of 752 guardsmen from the 101st Air Refuelling Wing (ARW) in Maine and the 108th ARW in New Jersey under a Presidential Selective Reserve Call-Up for Operation Allied Force.

June 4, 1999
Virginia ANG presented a proposal to the National Guard Bureau to relocate the 192nd Fighter Wing from Richmond to Langley Air Force Base and form a Virginia ANG associate unit to fly the F-22 Raptor as part of the 1st Fighter Wing when it received the aircraft.

June 18, 1999
Two Louisiana ANG F-15As from the 159th Fighter Wing that had deployed to Naval Air Station Keflavik in Iceland for a NATO exercise intercepted Russian Tu-95 Bear bombers that had penetrated the Icelandic Military Air Defence Identification Zone in a long-range probe not seen since the Cold War. Two more Louisiana ANG F-15s launched from Keflavik to escort the bombers out of the area.

June 20, 1999
NATO officially ended the air war against Yugoslavia, Operation Allied Force, after Serb forces completed their withdrawal from Kosovo.

June 21, 1999
A-10s assigned to the 104th Expeditionary Operations Group based at Trapani Air Base, Sicily, flew their final airborne close air support alert sorties for Operation Allied Force.

June 24, 1999
The ANG Crisis Action Team reported that the ANG had deployed 73 KC-135s and 18 A-10s for Allied Force operations as of this date.

July 27, 1999
The 135th Airlift Group of the 175th Wing, Maryland ANG, accepted the ANG's first brand new C-130J, 97-1351, at its home station of Martin State Airport.

October 1, 1999
The ANG and Air Force Reserve were integrated with the active-duty air force in the service's new Expeditionary Aerospace Force (EAF). The air force began implementing its EAF concept as the first of its ten Aerospace Expeditionary Forces (AEFs) began deploying overseas. This was known as AEF Cycle 1. The ANG had agreed to supply 10% of the planes and personnel for each AEF.

October 1, 1999
The first ANG pilot began flying with the 325th Fighter Wing at Tyndall Air Force Base, Florida, as part of a new programme in which the guard provided flight instructors to help train new active-duty F-15 pilots. The ANG associate unit was designated Detachment 1 of the Southeast Air Defense Sector.

January 13, 2000
Elements of the 169th Fighter Wing, South Carolina ANG, deployed from McEntire

ANG Base by commercial air to Incirlik Air Base, Turkey, to participate in Operation Northern Watch (ONW). It marked the first ANG unit to deploy operationally in the Suppression of Enemy Air Defenses (SEAD) role, the first ANG unit to employ the AGM-88 High Speed-Anti Radiation Missile in a SEAD mission and the first to deploy a female ANG F-16 pilot on an operational combat mission to ONW.

September 11, 2001

F-15s assigned to the Massachusetts ANG were scrambled from Otis ANGB, and ANG F-16s were scrambled from Langley Air Force Base, Virginia, to intercept hijacked commercial airliners bound for the World Trade Center in New York City and the Pentagon but arrived too late to thwart the terrorist attacks.

September 11, 2001

Shortly after the four airliners hijacked by terrorists in the US crashed, the Pentagon gave NORAD the operational lead to use USAF fighters to patrol the skies over more than 30 cities. US Navy fighters also flew off the Atlantic coast, near New York. Within hours of the terrorist attacks, 34 ANG fighter units had generated aircraft and were ready to fly combat

Above: **Mississippi ANG C-130H 90473 assigned to the 172nd Airlift wing takes off from the snow-cleared runway at Kulis Air National Guard Base, Anchorage in 1984.** US Air National Guard

missions. Fifteen of those units had flown 179 fighter missions during the first 24 hours. In addition, 18 ANG tanker wings had generated 78 missions.

September 14, 2001

Congress authorised use of the US armed forces against the terrorists who had attacked the country on September 11 and those who harboured them.

September 18, 2001

NORAD reported that ANG fighters continued to maintain continuous

combat air patrols over Washington, DC, and New York City because of the terrorist attacks on September 11. In addition, NORAD emphasised that a pair of ANG fighters were being maintained on alert at each of 26 locations to respond quickly to any new threats.

October 8, 2001

Four EC-130E Commando Solo aircraft from the Pennsylvania ANG's 193rd Special Operations Wing began broadcasting music and information to the Afghan people as part of Operation Enduring Freedom.

Continued on page 34

AIR GUARD HEAVY BOMBERS

An overview of the nine-years the B-1B strategic bomber served with the Air National Guard

Above: **Four B-1B bombers assigned to the Kansas Air National Guard's 18th Bomb Wing over the state of Georgia in 2002.** US Air National Guard

AIR COMBAT COMMAND transferred ten B-1B bombers to the Kansas Air National Guard on July 1, 1993, marking the first time a reserve component unit had control of a long-range bombers. The bombers were assigned to the 184th and 116th Bomb Wings based at McConnell Air Force Base, Kansas, and Dobbins Air Force Base, Georgia.

On May 27, 1993, the USAF had approved a series of force-structure changes at McConnell Air Force Base, near Wichita in Kansas. The 184th Fighter Group, which trained pilots for the F-16, relinquished 54 fighter jets for ten B-1B bombers and became the 184th Bomb Group. The aircraft involved were previously assigned to the resident 384th Bomb Wing, which deactivated as part of the base realignment from Air Combat Command to Air Mobility Command, hosting the KC-135R-equipped 22nd Air Refuelling Wing with 48 aircraft assigned.

Kansas and Georgia

Back in October 1962, the bomb group was converted to the 184th Tactical Fighter Group, when the 127th Tactical Fighter Squadron became the flying organisation assigned to it. In March 1971, the unit was redesignated the 184th Tactical Fighter Training Group and tasked with conducting academic and flight training of combat aircrews in the tactics, techniques and operations of fighter aircraft and associated equipment. Kansas ANG F-16 pilots underwent the standard five-month B-1B course at Dyess Air Force Base, which comprised 12 sorties. Maintenance crews began their initial training in January, followed by operational duties in March, when guard and active-duty crew chiefs began working together. The 184th completed its conversion at McConnell in FY1996. As an operational and fully deployable entity, readiness was the 184th's primary focus to enable it to conduct global strike missions anytime, anywhere.

The 116th BW began its conversion to the B-1B on April 1, 1996, relocating

to Robins Air Force Base, Georgia, during the year and completing the process in December 1998. The 116th BW assumed the bomber mission after more than half-a-century of flying fighters.

Transition from the B-1B

On June 26, 2001, Pentagon officials announced that Secretary of Defense Donald Rumsfeld proposed cutting the USAF's fleet of 93 B-1B bombers by nearly one-third. This meant the 116th and 184th Bomb Wings in Georgia and Kansas would lose their B-1Bs and their funding as of October 1, 2001.

On September 26, Secretary of the Air Force James Roche confirmed that Georgia ANG's 116th Bomb Wing would transition from B-1B bombers to E-8C joint surveillance target attack radar system aircraft and be redesignated the 116th Air Control Wing. Roche also confirmed that Kansas ANG's 184th Bomb Wing would transition from B-1B bombers to KC-135 tankers.

At Robins AFB, an aircrew assigned to the 116th Bomb Wing flew the unit's last scheduled B-1 training flight on June 22, 2002. On September 17, 2002, the last B-1 assigned to the 116th Bomb Wing of Georgia ANG departed Robins AFB for Davis-Monthan AFB, Arizona. At the time, the 116th was preparing to merge with Air Combat Command's 93rd Air Control Wing (ACW) to become the 116th ACW, the first blended wing in the USAF equipped with the E-8C battlefield surveillance aircraft.

At McConnell, the last B-1 assigned to Kansas ANG's 184th Bomb Wing departed the base on August 4. Seven weeks later, on September 16, 2002, the wing became the 184th Air Refueling Wing.

In 2007, the 184th ARW was notified it would lose its flying mission altogether and reorganise as the 184th Intelligence Wing. Consequently, it would increase its presence in cyber combat and gain other ground-based combat support missions, including command and control, munitions storage and air support operations. On August 1, 2019, the unit was renamed the 184th Wing to reflect its multi-faceted mission set.

Continued from page 31

Above: **KC-135E Stratotanker 80080 on an aerial refuelling mission of the UK sector of the North Sea for the 151st Air Refuelling Wing, Utah ANG.** US Air National Guard

December 2001
Rhode Island ANG's 143rd Airlift Wing became the first US military unit to be equipped with the brand-new C-130J-30 Hercules transport.

March 29, 2003
As of this date, the ANG had flown 72% of Operation Noble Eagle's fighter sorties, 52% of its tanker sorties and 35% of its airlift sorties.

December 17, 2003
In a ceremony at its plant in Long Beach, California, Boeing delivered the first of eight brand-new C-17A Globemaster IIIs to the Mississippi ANG's 172nd Airlift Wing.

February 27, 2004
On this date, the 107th Fighter Squadron, Michigan ANG, deployed ten F-16C aircraft on their AEF rotation to Iraq for Operation Iraqi Freedom. They were the first F-16 unit in the air force to operate from Kirkuk Air Base, a former Iraqi military installation. They employed the Theater Airborne Reconnaissance System pod developed by the ANG in actual combat conditions.

May 2, 2004
Tennessee ANG's 164th Airlift Wing in Memphis phased out the last C-141B, 60157, in the ANG inventory during a ceremony at its home station. The unit was slated to receive C-5s.

November 30, 2004
Headquarters, US Air Force approved an ANG request to establish the 170th Operational Support Squadron, Nebraska ANG. It would become an associate unit of Air Combat Command's 55th Wing, which conducts a wide variety of global reconnaissance, intelligence, information operations, command and control, presidential support, treaty verification, training and airlift missions from Offutt Air Force Base, Nebraska.

December 1, 2004
USAF officials announced that Virginia ANG pilots from the 192nd Fighter Wing at Richmond would be partnering with pilots from the Air Combat Command's 1st Fighter Wing to train on the F-22 Raptor, the service's newest fighter aircraft.

January 1, 2005
The 170th Operational Support Squadron, Nebraska ANG, was activated at Offutt Air Force Base, Nebraska, as an associate unit of the Air Combat Command's 55th Wing at Offutt.

March 23, 2005
The USAF took delivery of its final E-8C Joint STARS aircraft. It was the 17th production model of the aircraft, all of which were assigned to the blended ANG/active-duty 116th Air Control Wing at Robins Air Force Base, Georgia.

July 8, 2006
Lieutenant Colonel Steve Hopkins took command of the USAF's new 30th Airlift Squadron (AS) in a ceremony at Cheyenne, Wyoming. The 30th AS would come under the operational control of the Wyoming ANG's 153rd Airlift Wing and share the latter's C-130 transports. Administratively, the 30th would be attached to the 463rd Airlift Group at Little Rock Air Force Base, Arkansas. The 30th was the first unit of its kind associated with the ANG.

August 16, 2006
A ribbon-cutting ceremony at McConnell Air Force Base in Kansas opened the ANG's newest and largest intelligence facility. The $7.4 million development housed Kansas ANG's 161st Intelligence Operations Group.

November 28, 2006
The ANG formally established its first MQ-1 Predator-equipped unit at March Air Reserve Base, California, when the 163rd Air Refuelling Wing was redesignated the 163rd Reconnaissance Wing.

January 10, 2007
The first of eight C-21 executive transports arrived at Hector Airport, North Dakota, intended to serve as a bridge mission for the North Dakota ANG's 119th Fighter Wing as it relinquished its F-16s due to the 2005 Base Realignment and Closure process.

April 24, 2007
Ohio ANG's 178th Fighter Wing hosted a ceremony officially welcoming the Royal Netherlands Air Force to its Springfield-Beckley home station and celebrating the new joint US-Dutch F-16 pilot training programme.

April 8, 2008
In accordance with the 2005 BRAC law, the last A-10 Thunderbolt II aircraft assigned to the 118th Fighter Squadron, 103rd Fighter Wing, Connecticut ANG, departed Bradley ANGB.

June 18, 2008
Colonel Gregory Champagne, vice commander of 131st FW, and Major David Thompson, 131st FW, completed the first B-2 sortie flown and launched by Missouri ANG.

Continued on page 36

AIRBORNE BATTLE MANAGEMENT

The E-8C Joint Surveillance Target Attack Radar System in Air National Guard service

THE FINAL E-8C joint surveillance target attack radar system aircraft left Robins Air Force Base, Georgia, on November 15, 2023. In the time since the weapon system participated in Operation Desert Storm in 1991, the E-8C fleet conducted 14,259 operational sorties and amassed 141,169 flying hours. Ramstein Air Base in Germany was the location for the final E-8C operational sortie on September 21, 2023.

Georgia ANG's B-1B-equipped 116th Bomb Wing relocated to Robins AFB, Georgia in 1996, with 1,100 personnel assigned. In October 2002, the unit was re-designated the 116th Air Control Wing, flying the E-8C JSTARS airborne battle management, command and control, intelligence, surveillance, and reconnaissance aircraft. Its primary mission was to provide theatre commanders with ground surveillance to support attack operations and targeting that contributed to the delay, disruption, and destruction of enemy forces.

Boeing 707-300 airframes were extensively modified with the radar, communications, operations, and control subsystems required to perform the JSTARS operational mission. This included installing a 27ft long, canoe-shaped radome under the forward fuselage to house a 24ft APY-7 side-looking phased array antenna. Tiltable to either side of the aircraft, the antenna scanned a 120° field of view covering nearly 19,305 square miles, with the capability of detecting targets at a distance of 150 miles.

The E-8C was the only platform in the US DoD arsenal that combined accurate wide-area moving target detection with synthetic aperture radar imagery to locate, classify and track targets in all weather conditions from standoff distances. The system gathered and displayed detailed battlefield information on ground forces, which was relayed in near real-time to ground stations and C4I nodes.

Above: **E-8C Joint STARS 96-0042/ GA on a training sortie from Robins Air Force Base, Georgia.** US Air National Guard

The first E-8C Joint STARS aircraft to be retired from service, 92-3289/GA, arrived at Davis-Monthan Air Force Base, Arizona, on February 11, 2022, for storage with the 309th Aerospace Maintenance and Regeneration Group. US Air National Guard/Captain Ronald Cole

Continued from page 34

April 4, 2009
West Virginia ANG's 167th Airlift Wing was formally dedicated as a fully operational C-5 unit in a ceremony at Martinsburg, West Virginia.

April 27, 2009
Mississippi ANG's 186th Air Refuelling Wing took possession of the MC-12W, the USAF's newest ISR platform.

June 13, 2009
A ceremony was held at Lambert Field for more than 2,000 people to watch the launch of the last F-15Cs previously operated by Missouri ANG's 131st Tactical Fighter Wing. The aircraft were flown to Hickam Air Force Base in Hawaii for assignment to the ANG's 199th Fighter Squadron. With the send-off, flight operations at Lambert airport ceased after 86 years.

April 27, 2010
The first of 20 Block 50 F-16Cs landed at Duluth airport, home station of Minnesota ANG's 148th Fighter Wing, to replace the unit's Block 25 F-16s.

April-October 2012
The 104th Fighter Wing (131st Fighter Squadron), Massachusetts ANG, and the 159th Fighter Wing (122nd Fighter Squadron), Louisiana ANG, deployed 12 F-15Cs and more than 300 personnel to the Middle East. The last time ANG Eagles went to war was in September 2000, to help enforce the no-fly zone of southern Iraq in Operation Southern Watch.

October 1, 2013
Michigan ANG's 110th Operations Group officially stood up its MQ-9 Reaper organisation. The operations tempo for these crew members has remained steady throughout 2014 as they learned a new mission with an air vehicle physically located thousands of miles from their control stations.

September 19, 2019
Vermont ANG's 158th Fighter Wing received its first two F-35A Lightning II aircraft in South Burlington, Vermont on September 19, 2019. The 158th FW became the first ANG unit to operate the fifth-generation fighter jet.

April 21, 2020
In mid-April 2020, USAF leaders announced the decision to base F-35A fighters at Truax Field in Madison, Wisconsin, and Dannelly Field in Montgomery, Alabama. Truax is home to the Wisconsin ANG's 115th Fighter Wing, while Dannelly is home to Alabama ANG's 187th Fighter Wing.

June 8, 2021
USAF leaders announced that Ebbing ANG Base in Fort Smith, Arkansas, had been selected as the preferred location to establish an F-35A Lightning II training centre for foreign military sales participants. The decision would also lead to the move of the 425th Fighter Squadron, a Republic of Singapore F-16 training unit from Luke Air Force Base, Arizona. The new training centre has capacity for up to 36 fighter aircraft.

August and September 2021
Missouri ANG's 131st Bomb Wing led the first Bomber Task Force to Iceland. This was the first time B-2s had forward deployed to Keflavik Air Base, marking a significant event for capabilities between allied fighter jets and stealth bombers.

The B-2s integrated and trained with RAF Typhoon fighters and Royal Norwegian Air Force F-35As.

May 10, 2022
Eight F-35s assigned to Vermont ANG's 158th Fighter Wing landed at Spangdahlem Air Base, Germany on May 2 to support NATO's enhanced air-policing mission. The wing helped NATO patrol the skies along the alliance's eastern flank during a time of rising tension in Europe.

July 8, 2022
Two active-duty squadrons joined ANG wings in ceremonies on July 8. The 306th Fighter Squadron became an associate of New Jersey ANG's 177th Fighter Wing, while the 64th Air Refuelling Squadron activated under the auspices of New Hampshire's 157th Air Refuelling Wing.

June 24, 2022
The Department of the Air Force announced a plan to activate a C-130J Formal Training Unit (FTU) at Little Rock Air Force Base, Arkansas, on June 24. Four C-130Js will be assigned to the unit to help ANG crews gain the experience and knowledge needed to operate the C-130J. Arkansas ANG's 189th Airlift Wing already flies the C-130H FTU.

September 2022
Vermont ANG's 158th Fighter Wing welcomed Lieutenant Kelsey Flannery, the first female F-35 pilot in the ANG. It also marked the first training sortie between a country and a state ANG unit following the ratification of a state partnership programme. The agreement resulted in the 158th FW deploying F-35s to Zeltweg, Austria, during June 2023.

Below: **Two F-101B Voodoo aircraft assigned to the 107th Fighter Interceptor Group, New York ANG once based at Niagara Falls ANG Base.** US Air National Guard

September 30, 2022
Air Mobility Command grounded 116 H-model C-130s and variants on September 30 after discovering propeller-barrel cracks during depot maintenance at Warner Robins Air Logistics Complex, Georgia. Most of the aircraft were assigned to ANG and Air Force Reserve Command units.

November 21, 2022
A KC-46A Pegasus assigned to New Hampshire ANG's 157th Air Refuelling Wing flew a non-stop mission halfway around the globe on November 16-17. The point-to-point, 36-hour, 16,000-mile, multi-crew sortie was the longest such mission in the history of Air Mobility Command, the active-duty major command to which the 157th is aligned.

January 31, 2023
ANG airlift wings equipped with C-130H Hercules aircraft had enough operable aircraft to resume training following AMC's grounding on September 30, 2022. The NGB said the affected units have three C-130Hs with either the upgraded eight-blade NP 2000 propeller assembly or newly constructed legacy 54H60 propeller. USAF officials traced the issue to maintainers using the wrong tool to etch numbers on propeller barrels.

April 25, 2023
The USAF announced the recapitalisation plane for three ANG F-15 fighter units. The 144th Fighter Wing at Fresno ANG Base in California and the 159th Fighter Wing at Naval Air Station Joint Reserve Base New Orleans in Louisiana

will each receive 18 F-15EXs. The 104th Fighter Wing at Barnes ANG Base in Massachusetts will get 18 F-35As.

August 29, 2023
Arizona ANG's 162nd Wing will begin training Ukrainian pilots and maintainers on the F-16 Fighting Falcon at Morris ANG Base in Tucson, Arizona. The Arizona ANG unit has long been the US Air Force international F-16 schoolhouse. The Ukrainian programme includes a series of courses ranging from basic flight training to instruction on fighter fundamentals, weapons employment, combat manoeuvring and tactical intercepts, among other concepts.

September 19, 2023
The USAF announced on September 14, 2023, that it had tentatively selected the 103rd Airlift Wing in Connecticut, the 120th Airlift Wing in Montana, the 133rd Airlift Wing in Minnesota and the 182nd Airlift Wing in Illinois to convert from aging C-130H Hercules aircraft to the more advanced C-130J Super Hercules.

October 24, 2023
Plans to modify 54 ANG and 23 Air Force Reserve C-130H aircraft with the Avionics Modernization Program Increment 2 over a five-year period were announced by the USAF. Many of the ageing aircraft have already received new propellers, engines, wing boxes and communications to extend their lifespan.

January 12, 2024
Officials announced that the USAF had selected Michigan ANG's 127th Wing

based at Selfridge ANG Base near Detroit as its preferred location for the new home for 12 KC-46A Pegasus tankers. The new tankers are expected to begin arriving at the wing's 171st Air Refuelling Squadron in 2029, to replace eight KC-135R Stratotankers being retired from 2027.

March 7, 2024
An announcement by the USAF stated that Maryland ANG's 175th Wing will swap the unit's A-10C Thunderbolt II fighter mission for an expanded cyber mission. The 175th Cyberspace Operations Group already operates from Warfield ANG Base.

October 3, 2024
Seven ANG air refuelling wings are in the running to become the KC-46A Pegasus Main Operating Base 7 from 2031. The seven wings are Bangor ANG Base in Maine (101st ARW), Forbes Field ANG Base in Kansas (190th ARW), Key Field ANG Base in Mississippi (186th ARW), McGhee Tyson ANG Base in Tennessee (134th ARW), Rickenbacker ANG Base in Ohio (121st ARW), Scott Air Force Base in Illinois (126th ARW) and Sumpter Smith ANG Base in Alabama (117th ARW).

October 16, 2024
Missouri's ANG's 131st Bomb Wing participated in precision strikes against Houthi forces in Yemen on October 16, targeting five hardened underground weapons storage locations. Air Force Global Strike Command's 509th Bomb Wing also played a significant role in the strikes from Whiteman, as did the Joint-Global Strike Operations Center.

Above: **A large container being offloaded from a C-5A Galaxy from the 105th Airlift Wing, New York ANG at Entebbe International Airport, Uganda, during the international relief effort for Rwandan refugees.**
US Air Force

ALWAYS
READY

New York ANG's 105th Airlift Wing operates C-17A Globemaster IIIs on worldwide missions as tasked by Air Mobility Command

STEWART INTERNATIONAL AIRPORT is located to the west of the cities of Newburgh and Windsor in Orange County, 70miles north of New York City. The airport is home to New York Air National Guard's 105th Airlift Wing equipped with a small fleet of C-17A strategic transport aircraft. The site's military connection goes back to the mid-1930s, when it was developed as a US Army Air Force facility used for flight training of cadets from the US Military Academy West Point. The USAF closed the base in 1970. Thirteen years later, New York ANG's 105th Tactical Air Support Group moved in, equipped with Cessna O-2 Skymaster forward air control aircraft, the smallest type in USAF service. The following year, the 105th traded in its O-2 aircraft for the C-5A Galaxy strategic transporter. The wing has been resident ever since, re-equipping with the C-17A Globemaster III in 2011.

Current Operations

Explaining how the wing's aircraft and crews are tasked for a mission, Captain Jonathan Guagenti, a C-17 aircraft commander and chief of current operations for the 137th Airlift Squadron, said: "Our operations office receives the mission taskings from either Air Mobility Command's Tactical Air Control Center at Scott Air Force Base, Illinois, or from the National Guard Bureau, which are passed to our schedulers. Each quarter, we select what guard lifts [missions specifically flown in support of the US Army or ANG] and my office is responsible for all kinds of duties including planning the locations to be uses, contacting the FBOs for fuel and services and scheduling crew and transportation."

Chief of scheduling and a C-17 pilot, Captain Shania Kirnan, continued: "The operations office holds the three-month outlook, while the scheduling office holds a one-month outlook. Scheduling pilots is a challenge because so many of them are airline pilots who work specific schedules and don't always have the time to give up to the ANG. Many of our loadmasters work for organisations that are willing to let their people be a member of the ANG and fly missions with us. Typically, we look at the month ahead and post a schedule to our crews so they can compare their civilian schedule to their military schedule and bid for trips. We always have loadmasters available, but not so with pilots. From the scheduler's perspective, we use operational risk management to make sure the names that we're given meet the mission requirements to ensure the crew will be safe and effective.

"Typically, our missions run through Dover or McGuire to pick up the cargo and then head to Europe. Generally, those missions last about five to seven days, then the crew comes home. If the aircraft breaks down, they must start juggling their schedule, and if the aircraft is grounded for long enough, sometimes we must release the crew or some of the crew from the mission and get replacement crewmembers to continue with the aircraft for the entirety of the mission and back to Stewart."

Explaining cargo collection at an aerial port squadron, Staff Sergeant Kristen Mills, a loadmaster with the 137th Airlift Squadron, said: "We meet with someone from the port who has details of the cargo to be loaded on the plane and the load plan. We're the on-scene expert and if something needs to get moved for whatever reason, we're trained in knowing where it can go on the aircraft, to make sure that everything is balanced and safe to fly, then work with the load teams to get it on the aircraft and tied down. Though the load plan is formed a certain way, that doesn't mean we can't change things to best fit the cargo, depending on what location we go to first.

Below: **A C-17 Globemaster III assigned to the 105th Airlift Wing parked at Resolute Bay, Nunavut, Canada.** US Air National Guard/ MSgt Patrick Espeut

Above: **A C-17 Globemaster III from the 105th Airlift Wing on the ramp at Kuwait International Airport on June 30, 2023.** US Air National Guard/ Lieutenant Briana Ross

"Challenges with loading the aircraft are not so much the cargo, but the methodology of how you load the cargo, whether it's with a K-loader or a forklift. It depends on the nature of the cargo and how it's brought into the jet. So that requires additional attention to detail when loading certain things. A tank is probably one of our easier loads because it is driven on and off the aircraft. The complication behind that is the number of chains used to restrain the tank. One big factor is the time crunch. It's measured from the second that we land to the second that we must take off and lasts two hours and 45 minutes on the ground for the C-17. We can always go past that, depending on the nature of the cargo. Helicopters might take longer because they need to be winched onboard."

Operation Allies Refuge

Discussing notable missions flown with the 105th AW, Captain Guagenti recalled his involvement in Operation Allies Refuge, the US evacuation of Afghanistan: "Originally, I was supposed to fly to Guatemala and operate in Central and South America for a few days, but my crew was told that we'd be flying east, but they couldn't tell us what for. While we were packing, we were

Right: **Cargo pallets are loaded on to a C-17 Globemaster III from the 105th Airlift Wing during exercise Guerrier Nordique at Resolute Bay, Nunavut, Canada.** US Air National Guard/ MSgt Patrick Espeut

told to pack for at least ten days. We got news alerts about Afghanistan falling apart and put two and two together. I flew into Kabul three times during the evacuation. On the first night, we carried a Chinook helicopter with aircrew and a team from the 160th Special Operations Aviation Regiment based at Fort Campbell, Kentucky, but we didn't land because the Taliban had reached the outskirts of the city and people had flooded onto the runway. We returned on the second night with the Chinook and its team. We were later told that if we had not got that helicopter into Kabul, a second Chinook delivered the previous night would not be able to fly per the regiment's operational requirements. The two Chinooks wound up evacuating over 800 people from the countryside and around the city.

"For my second mission into Kabul, we evacuated 348 civilians, the youngest of which was a 17-day-old baby girl. The third time was to collect the 13 service members killed by the blast caused by a suicide bomber at Abbey Gate. We flew the fallen to Kuwait City, where we went

Right: **A crew chief assigned to the 105th Aircraft Maintenance Squadron works on the left wingtip of an aircraft with the aid of a custom designed C-17 maintenance platform.** US Air National Guard

into crew rest. At the end of crew rest, an active-duty aircraft flew the fallen back to Dover. We followed all the way to Dover as the back-up aircraft. The oldest of the 13 was 31, everyone else was 25 and under. Two weeks later, our maintainers found a bullet hole in the aircraft's winglet. So that was the first time I'd received damage to my aircraft from rifle fire.

"When we landed on the second night, the day after the runway was overrun by people, the airfield was still closed and we didn't have enough gas to hold, so started to leave the country, but our control agency called us by radio advising there was a tanker available. They advised us to get gas and return to the hold until the field was reopened.

"The aircraft commander conducted aerial refuelling over Pakistan, the Persian Gulf and all the way back to Kabul with 130,000lb of gas, so we were able to hold until the field was opened. We landed and made a left turn at the end of the runway, where the Taliban was located – we were not notified of that or that the United States had a security agreement. As we were taxiing back, we suddenly saw a group of trucks with headlights turned on. When I looked out the window using night-vision goggles, I saw a Taliban fighter up close for the first time. It was a surreal feeling to know that he could kill me at that point and there was absolutely nothing I could do about it. The field was completely dark. The airport was dark. There was garbage and suitcases everywhere and empty airplanes. It was a strange feeling being at the centre of something so historical and grand of a scale, and how small a part you play. It was overwhelming.

"Once the allied forces got control of the airport, it was relatively secure, but going in on the first night, no one knew what was going on. There were no tower controllers – they had all fled – so we were speaking to other airplanes trying to figure out the situation. A friend of mine was taking off from Kabul Airport on the first night and, as he went to rotate, he flipped his lights on just before colliding with a crowd that was on the runway.

"One of our aircrews flew multiple missions and evacuated 1,500 civilians. As rough and intense as it was for the aircrew, we were able to fly in and out. Compare that to the crazy situation faced by the troops who had to live at Kabul for two weeks and turn people away at the gates. I'm proud of what the C-17 community accomplished in such a dynamic situation, but amazed by the Marines, sailors and soldiers that were on the ground there."

Explaining his experiences as a crew chief with the 105th Aircraft Maintenance Squadron during the operation, Master Sergeant Michael Roe said: "The Afghan passengers were excited, but many were also scared because they had never been on an aircraft. The take-off was like a rollercoaster for them. Some kids were crying, but when the plane turned one way and then another way, they would laugh and cheer, which made the experience a great one. We had 400 people onboard. As they flooded onto the plane, we were trying to keep everybody standing up to get as many onboard as possible. Once the ramp was up and the doors closed, everybody could sit on the floor. We had straps going across rows of passengers.

The entire operation was eye-opening as to how bad it was for the Afghan people and made us realise how fortunate we are in the United States."

Commander's Overview

Colonel Kristopher Geis has held several key leadership positions in the New York ANG. He served as commander of the 105th Mission Support Flight, the 105th Aircraft Maintenance Squadron and as Chief of Staff for the 105th Airlift Wing. Today, Geis serves as the deputy wing commander.

Outlining the assets assigned to the 105th AW, Geis said: "We were the second ANG wing that transitioned to the C-17 and have nine C-17 aircraft assigned, one of only two ANG wings that have nine. The other four wings have eight, because there weren't enough aircraft to be transferred by the active-duty air force. However, we are only allocated enough personnel and equipment for eight; the ninth aircraft is additional.

"We have the 105th Base Defense Group, the only one in the ANG, comprising 300 military members who primarily work outside the wire in hostile areas, undertaking recovery and reconnaissance work. They train with the active duty 820th Base Defense Group based at Moody Air Force Base, Georgia.

"Our base defense group comprises three different squadrons: the 105th Security Forces Squadron, which provides security, checking people on and off the base, safeguarding our aircraft and maintaining the base perimeter; along with the 205th Base Defense Squadron and the 105th Security Support Squadron, which undertakes administration duties, ensuring that people are able to deploy and taking care of our security force structure.

"Another unique entity we have assigned is the 213th Engineering Installation Squadron, which is one of 13 such squadrons throughout the total force, all tied to US Space Command. This squadron specialises in engineering, installing and modifying ground-based communications, radar and aeronautical navigation systems here in the US and at deployed locations around the world."

Micro Veins and ATOMS

Outside of regular standard aircraft maintenance, the 105th Maintenance Group's commander, Colonel Matthew Brenner, explained a recent non-standard maintenance effort: "We volunteered to modify the first C-17 with micro veins. These are small aerodynamic devices installed on the tail of the aircraft. Several of our airmen went to Edwards Air Force Base in California and helped install the veins, but they were not involved in the flight testing. We're hoping to be part of a further evaluation that involves multiple aircraft fitted with micro veins to validate what fuel savings will be yielded if it's applied across the entire fleet. It's supposed to save about 1% fuel, but if the veins were applied to the whole fleet, it could save tens of millions of dollars in fuel over a year.

"We got a request from Boeing for a unit with aircraft availability to volunteer depending on its operations tempo. We had to consider how many aircraft we had available, the maintenance status of the aircraft and whether we had enough aircraft to support operations over the subsequent months. Fortunately, we had an aircraft available for the period defined and were still able to support our flying requirements."

Colonel Brenner also spoke of the Airlift Tanker Open Mission System

Right: **A US Army UH-60 Blackhawk helicopter loaded on to a C-17 Globemaster III assigned to the 105th Airlift Wing at Fort Drum, New York.** US Army

Below: **A C-17 Globemaster III assigned to the 105th Airlift Wing taking off from Resolute Bay, Nunavut, Canada.** US Air National Guard/MSgt Patrick Espeut

16TT - 94TT

(ATOMS), which is designed to advance the communications capability and interoperability of the C-17 with real-time secure communications system that the 105th AW operates. The programme is part of former AMC commander General Mike Minihan's 25x25 initiative to connect 25% of the mobility fleet by 2025. The ATOMS programme provides mobility crews with situational awareness and better survivability, upgrading communication abilities and in-flight internet access to enable a mobility aircraft to communicate with the joint force while airborne. The ATOMS system is housed on a roll-on, roll-off pallet.

Deployment

Last April, members of the 105th AW returned from a deployment to the US Central Command theatre. Colonel Geis explained: "It was the first time that we had deployed four of our aircraft and a group comprising aircrew and maintainers to conduct missions throughout the CENTCOM theatre. We were given two months' notice going into the 90-day deployment. Some airmen phased in and out on 45-day cycles. It allowed us to operate with more agility to drop off and pick up equipment.

"Our aircraft stayed in theatre. Typically, we play a transient role, fly into Germany and then to different locations from Germany, then back to Stewart. This time our four aircraft were there for 90 days, which was completely different – we'd had never had an exercise like that before. In accordance with the new Air Force Generation (AFFORGEN) model, Air Mobility Command tasked the reserve components, Air Force Reserve Command and the ANG in lieu of active duty.

Above: **The 9/11 commemorative C-17 Globemaster III flown by the New York ANG's 105th Airlift Wing at Stewart Air National Guard Base in Newburgh, New York, on October 14, 2023.** US Air National Guard/ TSgt Daniel Hotter

Below: **The winglet of a C-17 Globemaster III flown by the New York ANG's 105th Airlift Wing displays a logo commemorating the terrorist attacks on 9/11.** US Air National Guard/TSgt Daniel Hotter

"It really showed how well our maintenance group worked in tangent with our operations group and how they really looked after each other in that deployed environment. It was an event where the people involved will remember the great things they did to contribute to the larger operation that was going on at the time. Operating in the CENTCOM theatre also allowed our C-17s to be more agile, flying between regional locations to drop off or pick up equipment.

"The deployment was tasked by TRANSCOM through Air Mobility Command, which, as our MAJCOM, tasked ANG and reserve component wings under the AFFORGEN model. We were determined to put in the effort in lieu of the active duty. The first unit to deploy was the Air Force Reserve Command 445th AW based at Wright-Patterson Air Force Base in Ohio, which was given just two weeks' notice. We spoke with them about the pre-deployment bugs they experienced. We had two months to prepare to hopefully get it right. West Virginia

ANG's 167th Airlift Wing replaced us in accordance with the new cycle. For the 105th AW, this was the deployment phase of the AFFORGEN deployment model and followed the certification phase which included flying to Germany for Exercise Air Defender."

Explaining other aspects of the CENTCOM deployment, Captain Guagenti said: "The 105th AW was the first C-17 in the AFFORGEN model to take over the Operation Inherent Resolve mission at Al Udeid. We sent aircraft, pilots, loadmasters, crew chiefs, maintainers and security forces. Some of us stayed for the entire 90 days, while the others were able to split 45 days each thanks to the gracious agreements of the employers of our traditional guardsmen, to get them home in a reasonable timeframe."

Maintenance

Discussing some of the notable aspects of maintaining a C-17, aircraft hydraulics system specialist Senior Airman Casey Weiler said: "The flaps are large surfaces that we inspect during a home station check. Flaps must be configured properly, which means dropping them all the way down to make the hinge point accessible and visible. The largest surface we work on is the horizontal stabiliser – the entire surface moves to provide pitch trim; it's the largest moving surface on the plane. Working on the ramp, accessibility to the flight controls is a challenge.

"Every two-and-a-half years, we change the main landing gear's retraction hoses. We regularly inspect them as part of every home station check and typically notice a trend in repetitive replacement. That results in more frequent inspections and changing the items as needed.

Left: **Maintainers with the 105th Airlift Wing, New York ANG, perform repairs on a C-17 Globemaster III during Exercise Air Defender 2023 at Prestwick Airport, Scotland, on June 15, 2023.** Courtesy image

'The number one component that we repair and overhaul in the back shop here at Stewart is the main landing gear brakes. We completely strip them down, clean everything, discarding old packings and any other disposable items. Some items inspected are released if they're within parameters. We then reassemble the brake, bench-check it and turn it in as serviceable, ready to be fitted on the next plane."

Air Defence

Detailing the 105th's involvement in air defence, Colonel Geis said: "We sent 27 of our maintainers to Prestwick in Scotland complete basic maintenance on our planes and any other C-17s that landed there. Prestwick is a transient base for USAF C-17s flying back and forth between the US and Europe, which is a 24/7 operation.

"We were the first ANG airlift wing to stage personnel to a transient base and were proactive with the National Guard Bureau and Air Mobility Command to make sure we were not just staging our people at a base [Prestwick] most beneficial to the operation, but to participate in some of the exercise events.

"During Air Defender, three 105th AW aircrews performed one-third of all airlift missions throughout the exercise and the wing 22 missions in the deploy and redeploy phases. Crew chiefs and maintainers assigned to the deployment followed the multi-capable airman construct, with maintenance airmen performing traditional crew chief jobs such as refuelling aircraft, starting the APU, performing inspections with crew chief, and helping to change tyres."

"Fortunately, the retract hoses are easier to check for leaks. We install ground safety devices to prevent the gear from retracting, then pressurise the actuator without moving it – testing the hoses doesn't require the aircraft to be fully jacked like other landing gear maintenance procedures. The maintenance squadron typically takes the lead on jacking and most landing gear swinging. We [the AMXS] run the hydraulic mule and inspect and double-check our lines with a lot of pressure in them. More than half of the time we spend on checking is in preparation, making sure we follow the manual so there's no risk of injury.

Below: **The first C-17 Globemaster III assigned to the 105th Airlift Wing, lands at Stewart International Airport on July 18, 2011.** US Air National Guard

THAT OTHERS MAY LIVE

New York ANG's 106th Rescue Wing operates HC-130J Combat King aircraft and HH-60W Jolly Green II helicopters

WESTHAMPTON BEACH IS a village in Suffolk County on Long Island, New York, and the location of Francis S Gabreski Airport, a facility used by corporate and private aircraft and air taxi services. It is also the site of Francis S Gabreski Air National Guard Base, home of New York ANG's 106th Rescue Squadron. The unit is tasked with personal recovery, combat search and rescue – both federal missions when called to active-duty – and humanitarian causes such as hurricane relief.

offshore rescues and firefighting, which are state-governed missions. The wing's latest acquisition is the HH-60W Combat King II rescue helicopter, the latest generation of Sikorsky's H-60 series of combat rotorcraft.

Captain Ryan Fennell is an HH-60W pilot assigned to the 101st Rescue Squadron, who outlined the pilot training programme: "After undergraduate pilot training at Fort Rucker, Alabama, a student goes to Kirtland Air Force Base in New Mexico for their initial qualification on the HH-60W for six to nine months [the course at Kirtland is run by the 512th Rescue Squadron, a component of Air Education and Training Command's 58th Special Operations Wing].

"Post-Kirtland, a student is assigned to their unit – in this case, Gabreski – to start mission qualification training in the local area. They follow a syllabus and fly the first four flights with an instructor pilot. They are then released to fly with mission pilots. At that point they start to learn the airspace regulations and how they are expected to fly in a combat-coded squadron. This four-flight phase enables our squadron pilots to learn the students' strengths and weaknesses.

"From that point, student pilots will fly with mission capable pilots or flight leads and follow a syllabus working toward their successive upgrades to non-tactical mission pilot, then non-tactical aircraft commander, then full mission pilot. They complete numerous flights with instructor pilots to qualify for both the non-tactical mission pilot and non-tactical aircraft commander upgrades before they follow another specific syllabus to qualify as a mission aircraft commander. Flights are flown with an instructor in a two-aircraft formation. They fly a check ride to become an aircraft commander in the flight deck's 'dash two' position. Once the pilot has accrued time as an aircraft commander in the 'dash two' position, the squadron instructors then determine whether the student be considered for upgrade to flight lead. Once certified as a flight lead, they then work toward instructor and then evaluator."

An HH-60W crew comprises two pilots (an aircraft commander and a co-pilot) and two special mission aviators (SMAs) who are specialists with capable of multiple roles including pre-flight inspection, safe employment of weapons and defensive systems and in-flight maintenance of airborne weapons systems and associated equipment.

Explaining SMA training, Captain Fennell said: "They go through a training programme at Fort Rucker, Alabama, then go to Kirtland for their initial qualification course. Once a student returns to their unit, they fly local area mission qualification training (MQT) missions, comprising six flights with an instructor pilot which includes weapons training. Once they pass their MQT they are allowed to fly with no supervision. From that point, they undertake regular missions to gain experience until the squadron instructors recommend they are moved to an instructor role. They return to the schoolhouse at Kirtland to follow the training syllabus, returning to Gabreski as a qualified instructor. They can then work towards evaluator upgrade."

Right: **Top-down view of an HC-130J.** US Air Force

As an ANG unit with traditional guardsmen and full-time members assigned, one challenge for the wing is keeping their flight crews proficient in their tasks. Captain Fennell explained: "When any crew member returns from training, they are on full time orders for a minimum of three years. The wing does a good job of making sure some of our pilots stay here full time to solidify their craft and get comfortable enough in the aircraft, to the point where, if they have a civilian job to go back to, they can still pick it back up easily. With the HH-60W transition, a lot of our new pilots have been able to remain here full time to become proficient with the HH-60W before they return to their civilian jobs.

Below: **The third HC-130J Combat King II assigned to the New York ANG's 106th Rescue Wing on the flight line at Francis S Gabreski ANG Base, Westhampton, New York, in 2019.** US Air National Guard/ Airman 1st Class Kevin Donaldson

"Our pilots and SMAs who are not full-time and are unable to get those flying reps, have the self-discipline to study so that when they come here to fly, they're not starting at square one. Local people can come here and fly for one evening, and for people who live out of state, there's opportunities to go on TDY to complete individual training. To accomplish higher-level collective training, where we operate with other types of aircraft, we deploy to Volk Field, Wisconsin, and Savannah, Georgia.

"Our pilots, SMAs and maintainers generally serve here for many years, They take pride in the mission, and, in the case of our maintainers, they take ownership of their specific tail. We have good relationships with our

maintainers – they are hugely trusted, such that if one of them tells me something is wrong, there's no question. Additionally, the high crew resource management (CRM) intensity of this aircraft makes the working environment substantially better.

"I can tell from one of my SMA's inflection that if they say 'Break right' then I do it without question, because I have full confidence in all my crewmembers. When we're training at home station, crews are mixed and matched – you fly with anyone who is available. We select crews so that different people who use different techniques will show other crewmembers how different teams fly.

"When we deploy, the wing's leadership collaborates to build crews that they think will work well together. You will fly with that crew repeatedly throughout your deployment. Before deployment, we work through spin-up training, which is the best time to determine how those crews work together. If something's not meshing or something needs to change, leadership can swap people around, but a lot of the time, they do a really good job of building the crews.

"When deployed, you can easily fly more than 100 hours with the same people, so the CRM might not involve using the usual terminology, but you know exactly what's meant. Operating with the same crew – dubbed a hard crew – enables you to discuss methods with everyone on the same page. When you return from deployment, you start flying with other SMAs who may use different terms, which makes you think for a bit but quickly realise it's not the crew you were previously deployed with, but it works well. Mixing crews in the training environment helps identify best practices, strengths, and weaknesses, which are great for debriefs. Conversations in debriefs are oftentimes humbling, but everyone has the common

goal of getting better, whereas on deployment it's game time."

Whiskey Transition

The first cadre of eight pilots assigned to the 101st RQS went through the HH-60W transition course with the 41st RQS at Moody AFB in Georgia starting in late September 2024. They returned to Gabreski in November, with the cycle repeated until the end of January, when the last class started the course at Moody.

By that time, the 101st RQS had its full complement of HH-60W helicopters and maintainers assigned to the 106th Maintenance Squadron that were fully qualified on the 'whiskey'. As the pilots qualified on the type, the 101st RQS started flying mission qualification training sorties. Because the HH-60W has significantly more systems and automation compared to the HH-60G, it presents pilots with a steep learning curve, especially with the hand controls.

Above: **The view from a window of an HC-130J Combat King II search and rescue aircraft at 500ft over the Atlantic on June 21, 2023, while the crew searched for the *Titan* submersible, which went missing while diving on the wreck of the *Titanic*.** US Air National Guard

Below: **The third HC-130J Combat King II delivered to the 106th Rescue Wing rolls-out after landing at Francis S Gabreski ANG Base.** US Air National Guard/ Airman 1st Class Kevin Donaldson

Maintenance

Unlike the HH-60G, the HH-60W's systems are all integrated, whereas on the earlier type you had a lot of separate boxes trying to interface with each other. Consequently, the avionics shop has to understand different troubleshooting methodology and learn what goes where.

MSgt Jordan Butler is a helicopter maintenance technician and crew chief assigned to the 106th Aircraft Maintenance Squadron who maintains the airframe, rotor system and drive system. He said crew chiefs with the Gabreski-based wing spend three weeks learning the differences in airframe techniques and servicing.

Explaining the crew chief role with the HH-60W, MSgt Butler said: "Crew chiefs conduct daily maintenance and 40-hour inspections, and the phase inspection interval is currently set at 42 days. The HH-60G was equipped with the Integrated Vehicle Health Management System (IVHMS), on the HH-60W the IVHMS is integrated into the aircraft – there are more sensors, so there are more data points and, consequently, more data is generated. For certain faults that's great, but in other areas you still need a person to look for broken wires chafing or similar. But maintaining an HH-60W is not easier than an HH-60G, because soundproofing covers a lot of the components that we need to inspect, so you have to remove more panels to access different parts."

Combat Search and Rescue Training

Training for the combat search and rescues (CSAR) role is a tough challenge because of the variety of missions, so there's no one-size-fits-all programme. Major Christopher Aviles, an HH-60W pilot with the 101st Rescue Squadron, explained: "That's what makes our mission unique. We need to be available, ready, and trained to execute with no

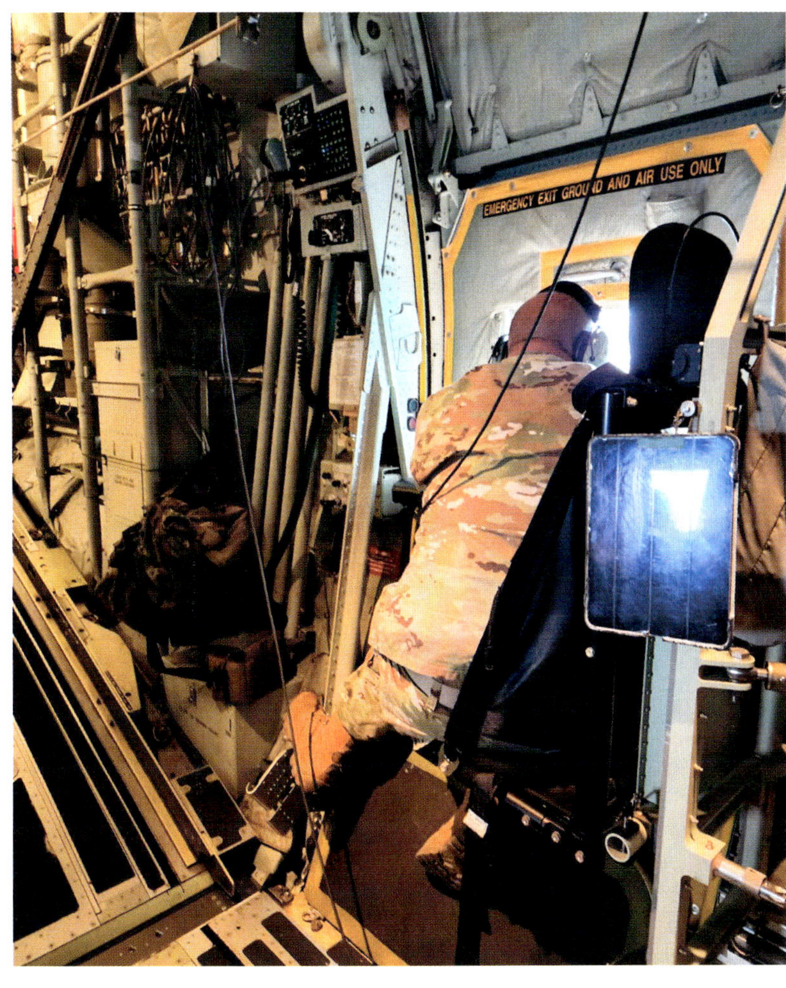

Left: **An airman scans the Atlantic Ocean from a window of an HC-130J Combat King II search and rescue aircraft for the *Titan* submersible on June 21, 2023.** US Air National Guard

notice in a wide variety of complex mission sets. We use simulation to good effect. The USAF has equipped different ranges with systems that simulate scenarios we would see on the battlefield, including smokey SAMs. When flying, we can also replicate ground fire, surface-to-air missiles, and pop-up targets to shoot at. We went to Volk Field in Wisconsin, which has a range where you can swivel the gun while flying to engage a pop-up target. Depending on the range, we can engage stationary targets, moving targets and moving pop-up targets."

Captain Fennell added: "We stage our TDYs so that each one has a different objective or a different scenario. We've participated in Red Flag exercises with involvement in the mission planning cycle and integration with the large strike package. Red Flag scenarios involve high-end threat environments and involve all types of assets. This provides one of the highest and most complicated ways that CSAR can be presented to aircrews.

With that as a baseline, we can step the threat level to something encountered in Afghanistan or Iraq versus a peer environment. That teaches us how to work with an air force strike package, which is hugely complicated. Then we can step it down to scenarios involving just us and the HC-130s going to point A to pick up person X, so our instructors can build up the scenarios to enable the younger guys to experience different types of mission sets and a variety of complexities. That way, both your most experienced and inexperienced personnel get to push the envelope, but in a controlled environment.

"Reaching a level of training that reflects the reality of a CSAR pick-up is achieved by using control measures such as mission complexity, training in the local area – to get comfortable with flying the aircraft, then to get used to employing the aircraft tactically, then to operate as a two-ship, then at night, then in one of the most challenging environments at Nellis, involving mountains and high-density altitude. At each step you can identify the risk and remain safe. If people are feeling uncomfortable, you knock it off and then discuss the situation at the debrief. With those reps, you become more experienced in a tactical, real-world environment by falling back on your training. Because you've done it so many times, although the threat is there, it's mitigated by your experience.

"Operating at 500ft and below on dark nights in a peacetime training scenario can be more uncomfortable than encountering enemy activity. Even flying just ten miles away, over the ocean with waves, fog, and no visible horizon, is very challenging. In such a scenario you should feel uncomfortable until the point where it becomes unsafe, but we do a good job of balancing that. Whenever I've been sweating and really stressed flying the HH-60, it has always been caused by the environment, whether that's weather rolling in, a dark night, a brownout, or a combination of all three."

Pararescuemen

USAF pararescuemen (PJs) who recover and medically treat downed military personnel take part in every aspect of a mission. PJs are skilled parachutists, scuba divers and rock climbers, as well as being arctic-trained. At Gabreski, Staff Sergeant Evan Vannieuwennhuyze serves as a PJ with the 103rd Rescue Squadron and is constantly training to develop, adapt and be ready to respond.

Below: **An HH-60G Pavehawk helicopter from the 106th Rescue Wing aerial refuels over eastern Long Island.** US Air National Guard/ Airman 1st Class Kevin Donaldson

He said: "We frequently undertake full mission profile exercises that involve all the components of mission planning and mission execution, so that we practice in different scenarios.

"During mission planning, as a medic I look at all aspects of potential injuries and pose questions such as how long has the person been out there and have they been fed? We prepare our gear and the equipment we foresee as necessary for the operation and the type of insertion method, rigging the helicopter to suit. We attend a briefing given by the team leader, who talks through the plan and how we're going to execute the mission.

"On the flight to the pick-up, we get in the mindset and go through the procedures. In some scenarios, you might have comms with the person while en route to them and sometimes you don't, but there are procedures to follow for specific scenarios. If you go down on a hoist, you're by yourself, or else you can go in with a team if necessary. You assess the casualty, apply life-saving treatment and package the patient on a SCAD if they're ambulatory, while always being aware of any time constraint. You take direction from your team lead and commanders, move to the location and get the person loaded on the helicopter, then head out."

HC-130J Combat King II

The Gabreski-based 102nd RQS operates the HC-130J Combat King II to support all mission sets held by the wing. Captain Chris Colwell is an HC-130J instructor pilot assigned to the 102nd RQS who described elements of its operations: "PJs are part of our rescue package for a civilian scenario – for example, rescuing a boat adrift in the water or somebody lost at sea. In either scenario, an HC-130J will air-drop PJs close to the person or boat. Our PJs can provide direct medical attention to somebody in need. For example, we've completed a couple of rescues for a stranded boat roughly 2,000 miles off the coast by launching with a team of PJs, recovered the person and prevented them from dying at sea.

"We drop a folded boat with an engine on the back, along with the PJs either with it or behind it. PJs unfold the boat in the water, turn it over, inflate it and then use the boat to reach the person in the water. The boat allows the PJs and any casualties to survive in the water before being picked up by another vessel. We usually air-drop a team of four PJs.

"On a search mission, we like to load as much fuel on the aircraft as we possibly can, bearing in mind weight restrictions for take-off and performance. The crew chief has procedures for loading the maximum amount of fuel in the aircraft, which enables more time in the air and more fuel to give away to the helicopters. The longer you can stay on station, you potentially increase the possibility of saving somebody's life. All kinds of fuel calculations are made for the HC-130J and the helicopters to determine how long we can stay on station, what quantity of fuel we need to get back home and determining the options for landing elsewhere if necessary. The bingo fuel state determines when we return home – once we see that number on our fuel gage, it's time to go. If we don't have helicopters with us, we can climb up higher to save our fuel burn and travel a lot farther. We can drag our helicopters from Long Island to a point 2,000 miles away, refuelling them along the way. It's an awful thing to be sitting in the helicopter for that long, but you have the potential to save lives.

"Our last call-out was for the *Titan* submersible accident in June 2023. We got the notification to commence the search and rescue, but didn't have a lot of information when we launched. Our assumption was that when the submersible was unable hold

Above: **An HC-130J Combat King II assigned to New York ANG's 106th Rescue Wing sits at Campo Grande in Brazil following a search and rescue training mission with the Brazilian Air Force during Exercise Tapio.** US Air National Guard/Airman 1st Class Sarah McKernan

Left: **Special mission aviators inside an HH-60G Pave Hawk helicopter search for a simulated isolated person during an event at Avon Park Air Force Range, Florida.** US Air Force

pressurisation, an emergency procedure automatically rose it to the surface. The crew's main concerns were fuel endurance, weather and how we would get the individuals out of the water. When we arrived on scene, it was completely fogged out with a very low cloud deck, so we went as low as 300ft above the water, trying to find this vessel on the surface. But, as we all know, it had been lost.

"We flew in the fog aided by nav equipment and had extra people onboard looking outside to increase the chance of finding the vessel. The flight out lasted three-and-a-half-hours at high altitude, then we descended and remained on station for about four hours before we had to return home, which took closer to four hours. The wind had pushed us along on the outbound leg, but we were fighting the winds when returning home."

Technical Sergeant James Casello, a crew chief with the 106th Aircraft Maintenance Squadron, described his role: "Adaptability and flexibility are the two leading qualities a person needs to be a crew chief. Things are always changing, and you don't expect things to break when they do, so you must flex to such events and adapt when other aircraft are not available. You must deal with what you've got, and fix things faster than you thought. It's up to us find and rectify the problem before calling for further help.

"Upon the aircraft's return, you complete a post-flight inspection, looking at the write-ups, briefing with the crew – especially as the computers that we debrief with may not advise on things the crew experienced on the aircraft itself and vice versa. The crew will report a good flight to you, but when you run the debrief, you might see advisories. You may still have an action that needs to be made, even though the occurrence wasn't tracked throughout the flight. You don't know what you're

Below: **Four HH-60G Pave Hawk search and rescue helicopters prepare for a mission during Exercise Agile Rage 2024 at Francis S Gabreski ANG Base on February 29, 2024.** US Air National Guard/ Senior Airman Sarah McKernan

103rd RQS assigned the PJs, collectively known as the rescue triad, supported by the 106th Operational Support Squadron, which cares for records and equipment.

Explaining the group's missions, Colonel Canette said: "CSAR is focused on rescuing downed aviators located behind enemy lines or the recovery of pilots who have been shot down or punched out for mechanical reason. Personal recovery includes non-combatant evacuation operations, MEDEVAC, CASEVAC and hostage recovery. Day-to-day, we focus on CSAR, which involves HC-130Js, HH-60Ws and PJs, because it's the most complicated and usually takes place in a hostile environment. It involves a tremendous amount of mission planning and a lot of tactics development and practicing to getting it right. The CSAR skill set translates very well into personal recovery."

On April 24, 2017, seven airmen assigned to the 106th RQW jumped into the night sky over the Atlantic Ocean, 1,700 miles from Long Island. Their mission was to provide emergency care for two sailors on the Slovenian bulk carrier *Tamar*, who had been badly burned in an explosion in the engine room. On June 4, 2022, during a ceremony at Francis S Gabreski ANG Base in Westhampton Beach, two combat rescue officers and five pararescuemen

trying to find, so rectification comes down to your troubleshooting.

"We have a diagnostic system that presents fault codes, which we use in reference to the maintenance publications, which give step-by-step instructions. Did it fix it? No. Now do this. Did that fix it? Yes. No further troubleshooting required. Or it may advise you to replace a specific part or repair a circuit or provide an advisory of what it has detected and what you need to do to fix it."

Staff Sergeant Owen Williams, a loadmaster with the 102nd Rescue Squadron, explained that role on the HC-130J: "On a rescue mission, we load different things: boats, life rafts, PJs and the rigging to set up for the air-drop. Those are all easy to load, depending on their size. If we are launched on alert, the time to take-off is crucial, so we call on the crew chiefs to help with loading and configuring the cargo hold. Boats are loaded in different configurations – sometimes they are inflated with the engine fitted, ready to go, sometimes they are folded up in a bundle and, once it's in the water, the PJs inflate it. There is plenty of clearance on either side when it goes out the back.

"When launched for a rescue, we run to the plane – the crew chiefs will already have the aircraft open and configured. We turn on the plane's power, load whatever is required and check the inventory. The crew chief makes sure the powered-up systems look good, then carries out visual inspections of the engines, the wheel wells and everything inside the aircraft. They do

their inspection, and we do ours to back each other up. The pilots also complete an inspection."

Operations Group

The 106th Operations Group, commanded by Colonel Jeff Canette, comprises four squadrons: the 101st RQS operating the HH-60W, the 102nd RQS flying the HC-130J Combat King II, the

Above: **Airmen from the 106th Maintenance Group repair an HC-130J during agile combat employment training on February 29, 2024.** US Air National Guard/ SSgt Kevin Donaldson

from the wing's 103rd Rescue Squadron were awarded the Air Force Commendation Medal for heroism for their actions in the mission. They were Lieutenant Colonel Edward Boughal, Major Marty Viera, Master Sergeant Jordan St Clair, Senior Master Sergeant Erik Blom, Master Sergeant Jedediah Smith and Staff Sergeant Michael Hartman.

Colonel Cannet piloted the HC-130 on the mission and said: "The complexity in that mission just can't be overstated. The fact that these guys had to do that, out there, alone and unafraid, was just a testament to their skill and ability.

"I got the call that a 625ft vessel traveling from Baltimore to Gibraltar had suffered an explosion 1,700 miles off the east coast of New York. Four seamen were critically injured and required immediate medical care. The 106th could not formally be assigned the *Tamar* rescue because it was a civil search and rescue mission. However, all the airmen involved volunteered to go on the flight. Before they could take off, the team needed to gather medical and surgical equipment from local hospitals. Then, aircraft maintenance issues threatened to end the mission shortly after take-off, but the flight engineers mitigated the problem.

Right: **Pararescuemen assigned to New York ANG's 103rd Rescue Squadron watch the arrival of an HC-130J Combat King II to transport patients during a personnel recovery training exercise.** US Air National Guard/TSgt Daniel Farrell

Right: **New York ANG airmen from the 106th Rescue Wing inspect a new HH-60W Jolly Green II search and rescue helicopter on September 12, 2024.** US Air National Guard/ Captain Cheran Campbell

Left: **A Zodiac inflatable boat leaves the aft ramp of a C-17 during a joint training operation conducted with members of the 103rd Rescue Squadron of New York ANG during Exercise Sentry Aloha.** US Air National Guard/SSgt Christopher Muncy

"The jump into the Atlantic at night involved dropping equipment bundles on target, along with two inflatable Zodiac boats. Once in the water, the pararescue team had to climb into the Zodiacs, retrieve the floating supplies, head to the ship and board the *Tamar* on a rope ladder while 15ft waves tossed the boat up and down."

Master Sergeant Jordan St Clair, the team leader, took up the story: "Every aspect of the mission presented challenges. Along with the distance and the jump, once on board, the airmen had to conduct emergency surgery, provide medical care for three days as the ship approached the Azores, then ensure the victims were airlifted onto a Portuguese helicopter. We were able to make a difference in the lives of two men. Those two men are alive and enjoying life today because of our ability to provide a capability that very few organisations can."

Discussing the scenario, Colonel Cannet said: "The crewmembers who were working in the engine room suffered from burns and issues with breathing. Their colleagues were doing CPR to try to keep them alive while we were en route.

We dropped 400lb of saline solution to be able to pump enough fluids into them to treat their burn wounds for a for about a day-and-a-half before they could reach Lajes in the Azores.

"We dropped a team of seven PJs, who conducted round-the-clock operations. They worked shifts once they realised they would be onboard for a while because the ship was too far away for helicopters to get out to and there were no other surface vessels in the area. Normally, we get folks to higher level medical care as fast as possible. But in the case of the *Tamar*, there was no other option than to ride it out on the ship until it could get into the Azores.

"We usually get about 3,000 miles of range out of an HC-130H, but on that trip we went about half that distance just to get to the scene, remain there while the teams got their Zodiacs inflated, got in the boats and dropped the bundles. Once they were aboard the *Tamar* we had to leave and recover to the closest airfield, which on that night was St John's in Newfoundland. It was a tough mission."

At the time of writing the 106th Rescue Wing had saved 2,974 lives.

SKI BIRDS AND

New York ANG's 109th Airlift Wing operates the LC-130H, a unique version of the Hercules aircraft fitted with skis

Above: **A ski-equipped LC-130H from the New York ANG's 109th Airlift Wing takes off from a ski way in Antarctica.** US Air Force

THE CITY OF Schenectady in eastern mid-state New York is where the General Electric Company was founded by Thomas Edison and where the American Locomotive Works once made stem and diesel locomotives to transport passengers and freight across the country. Today the city is still home to a General Electric research and manufacturing facility. To the northeast of downtown on the east side of the Mohawk River is Schenectady County Airport, home since May 1956 to the Stratton Air National Guard Base and the 109th Airlift Wing equipped with a fleet of LC-130H aircraft, a modified version designed with the capability to land on ice fields.

Dubbed 'ski birds', the fleet comprises ten aircraft: LC-130H2s, LC-130H3s and LC-130L2s. The oldest dates from 1973 and the newest from 1992. The fleet also includes two C-130H 'wheel birds' used for training and the wing is trying to acquire two more, operated by the 139th Airlift Squadron, the flying component of the 109th AW.

Outlining the squadron, Lieutenant Colonel Nate Dickinson, chief pilot with the 139th AS, said: "We have 60 pilots in our squadron – about 20 full time and the other 40 are part time guardsmen who come here for drill weekends and also deploy with us. As chief pilot, my responsibilities include dealing with training, staffing, retirements, pay and the things required by aircrew to complete their missions. Our cadre of pilots comprises co-pilots, ski aircraft commanders, instructors and evaluator pilots each with different training roles.

"All our ski birds are now fitted with NP2000 propellers and we're in the process of converting the T56 engines to the 3.5 version, which features an upgraded turbine section that generates 20% more power. At some higher altitude camps, the 3.5 version has the same limitations as the T56. Eight of our birds have been converted.

"An LC-130 is equipped with skis and fairings on the outside, a higher capacity hydraulic system that's required to power the skis, a hydraulic fluid reservoir with double the capacity of a standard reservoir, a fuel system equipped with valves so we can move fuel around and upload gas on the ground, a capability that regular slicks can't do. The skis are integral to the structure of the main landing gear: a slick bird has a strut in between the two wheels, on an LC-130 that's removed, and the ski is

WHEEL BIRDS

Skis

installed in its place – it essentially ties the two struts together.

"When we land on a paved runway, we perform a wheels-down, ski up landing. The pilot must be careful in a heavy crosswind because there's only eight inches of clearance between the bottom of the ski and the runway. With more weight loaded on the aircraft, the tyres squash down, reducing the clearance. The pilots must also be very careful not to over-rotate during take-off to avoid striking the backs of the skis on the ground.

"The skis and the landing gear can move independently – the wheels protrude through the bottoms of the skis. During a wheels-down, ski down landing on snow or ice, the wheels form part of the surface area of the ski, in the middle area."

Fairings are unique to the ski birds because the main wheels don't retract all the way up into the fuselage as per a regular Hercules. They retract a little bit less and pull the skis up with them. Together, the skis and the fairings act as the gear door – they retract to four inches of the bottom of the ferry and seal with a gasket.

The nose gear on an LC-130 functions with a pendulum action and swings forward. The mechanism is complex – if the ski was just fastened to the gear, the nose ski would protrude up through the front of the fuselage. A rigger strut keeps the nose ski parallel to the fuselage, so as the nose wheel moves up in its normal motion when the gear is raised, the nose ski just tucks up to the front of the fairing – it moves forward and up and acts as the door. Each ski weighs

about 2,500lb empty and a nose ski weighs about 800lb for a total of about 6,000lb added to the empty weight of the aircraft.

The skis operate on a cantilever system, hydraulically powered for raising and lowering the skis to land on snow or the wheels to land on a firm surface. The hydraulic rams are located inside and have in-built suspension, known as an air spring. It takes most of the suspension of the C-130 – there's little support from the OLEO strut. The air springs rotate and act as suspension otherwise you'd shake the teeth out of everybody when landing on the snow when the skis are lowered. There are two air springs on either side, so when the skis are lowered, the air springs rotate, enabling the aircraft to land on the skis. When parked on the flight line, the ski settles about six inches.

Once hydraulic pressure is placed on the plane and the engines are started, the ski will suck right up to the ferry, close to where it normally sits, about eight inches higher.

In training, if a new pilot executes a heavy pull off, the backs of the ski could strike the runway, especially in a crosswind situation, so they conduct benign take-offs to avoid scraping the skis. Occasionally, sacrificial scrape marks are left on the skis, but their strength helps to protect the aircraft's aluminium skin.

Skis have a lot of grease points that must be kept well-greased, the hinge points need to be maintained and, if a tyre change is performed, the skis create a lot of extra work. It takes about a day to take everything apart, get the jack out of the ski and move the ski out of the way to change the tyres. On a standard C-130H, a tyre change takes about an hour.

The skis are a box beam design, with a rectangular cross section that houses 20 electrical switches, four hydraulic actuators, a couple of valves and a lot of bracing and webbing. The aircraft are fitted with their original skis and the squadron is aware that nobody produces them anymore. They are continuously overhauled and refurbished in accordance with the maintenance life cycle. Skis add an extra hour to the pre-flight checks and much more time for anything that's gear or tyre related.

At the front of the aircraft, there is a panel for overriding the ski system. In the event of an emergency, the skis can be raised to enable a wheels-up landing. If there is an emergency with the landing

Above left: **An LC-130 Hercules aircraft from the 109th Airlift Wing sits at Summit Station, Greenland.** US Air National Guard/Senior Airman Jocelyn Tuller

Above right: **Pilots from the 109th Airlift Wing landing an LC-130 Hercules aircraft on a ski way in Greenland on May 9, 2024.** US Air National Guard/Senior Airman Jocelyn Tuller

gear system on a standard C-130 it's designed to neutralise hydraulic pressure and allow the landing gear to fall. With the LC-130, the emergency system is used to raise the skis. If that fails, a metal bar prevents the ski from coming all the way down and dipping forward.

When the skis are down on the snow, the nose wheel steering is not actuated. The aircraft can be likened to a 20,000hp snowmobile and differential power is used to casters the aircraft around. When on the snow, the flight engineer is allowed to move the throttles, because the co-pilot is busy doing other things. It requires implicit trust, good communication and a lot of training.

The aircraft has normal wheel landing gear controls and independent ski controls. Before every landing and

Above: **An LC-130 arrives at Resolute Bay, Nunavut, Canada on March 7, 2023, providing tactical airlift support for Guerrier Nordique 2023, a joint forces exercise.** US Air National Guard/ SSgt Madison Scaringe

take-off, the crew completes a triple concurrence check on the locations of all landing gear and ski system components to avoid a landing on a paved runway with the skis down.

Navigation and Other Systems

Discussing navigation for an LC-130, Major Marshall Clark said: "Until June 2024, we were still conducting celestial navigation with a sextant. Now we have a self-contained navigation system comprising two ring laser gyro INS and a single, four channel GPS. All external INS and GPS inputs provide a steering solution. The navigator, who sits at the back of the flight deck, manually inputs all data into the computer. It's not like a typical flight management system [FMS] with a worldwide database, but one that depends on the navigator to manually input latitude and longitude way points."

Explaining the systems installed in an LC-130'S cargo cabin that differ from a standard C-130H, Lieutenant Taylor Richards, a former loadmaster, said: "The LC-130H has a bigger winch, which is used for lifting pallets and cargo off the snow. Because of the squadron's ice field mission, we do a lot more winching of cargo than a standard C-130 squadron. Most of the places we go to don't have material handling equipment. Generally, we collect a single pallet, so we taxi the aircraft up to the pallet and winch it onto the aircraft. It's the only option because there's no forklift available or a snowmobile to tow the pallet out to the plane. We extend the winch out to the pallet, hook it up and put snow on the skids to make it easier to slide onto the aircraft. We're the only unit in the world that does that. Consequently, the loadmasters do a lot more work to load and secure the pallet on the plane.

Below: **An LC-130 Hercules aircraft from the 109th Airlift Wing sits at Raven Camp, Greenland on May 9, 2024.** US Air National Guard/ Senior Airman Jocelyn Tuller

An LC-130 at Resolute Bay in Canada during the joint forces exercise Guerrier Nordique 2023. US Air National Guard/SSgt Madison Scaringe

Below: **An LC-130 at Pituffik Space Base, Greenland, on May 12, 2023. The installation, previously Thule Air Base, was renamed in April 2023 to recognize Greenlandic cultural heritage.** US Air National Guard/ SSgt Madison Scaringe

"We're also the only unit left that still performs JATO or rocket-assisted take-offs, which we occasionally use in particular weather and ski way conditions. We use eight solid rocket fuel motors strapped to mounting points on the plane for additional thrust if required. The rockets are mounted, checked and wired up. The system provides 1,000lb of thrust per bottle, so about 8,000lb of thrust for approximately 15 seconds once ignited. JATO provides the equivalent thrust of one engine, so we have the equivalent of a fifth engine for the 15 seconds that it's running.

"The flight engineer hits the ignition button at the direction of the aircraft commander. The rockets provide just the power you need to get us past what we call the 'stagnation point', accelerating until we can lift off a ski way or an open snow area to get airborne. No one's making the bottles anymore – they cost $28,000 a bottle, so we don't use them all the time. A lot of our pilots haven't used them or have only operated the system a couple times in their entire career."

Ice Tasking

The 109th AW operates in two theatres: the Arctic and the Antarctic. In the northern hemisphere's summer, the wing deploys to Greenland to support the National Science Foundation (NSF). Operations in Greenland are split 50/50 between training and missions for the NSF. Five two to three-week deployments are made to Greenland throughout the summer.

Missions to Antarctica take place during the northern hemisphere's winter. The NSF puts in a request for support to the US Department of Defense (DOD). The Antarctica Treaty System, signed by the 12 nations active in the continent, bans military activity except to provide support to science efforts.

Explaining the deployment process, Lieutenant Colonel Dickinson said: "Once we are tasked by the DOD, we are assigned to a joint task force under the 15th Air Force in Hawaii. We leave Stratton with five aircraft in mid-October, on a journey that takes a week to fly via the US West Coast, Hawaii, Pago Pago and then Christchurch, New Zealand, which is where the US programme is based. McMurdo is our forward operating base where we stay for the duration of our deployment, but we undertake heavy level maintenance at Christchurch.

"McMurdo is on the Ross Ice Shelf. It has an ice ramp, an ice runway and a ski way. There are two airfields: Phoenix, which is considered an ice runway, and Williams

Above: **An LC-130 over Baffin Bay in Greenland.**
US Air National Guard/SSgt Madison Scaringe

Field, which is a ski way. Other nations and operators, such as Kenn Borek Air with its Twin Otters under contract to the NSF, also fly in and out of Williams Field. We use Phoenix as a divert field, depending on the time of the season and the condition of the ski way. They're only seven miles apart.

"We're self-contained down there, comprising an operations unit and usually five crews. That's the case in 2025 and we'll fly six days a week, with a typical schedule involving both day and night missions. We try to maintain flying operations around the clock. In recent years, the camps we fly to provide material handling, handling of equipment or firefighting equipment, even food.

"Our missions cover about half the continent, and each is dependent on the science that's going on and the logistics involved. In past years, we've been flying to the West Antarctic ice shelf, including the South Pole, which as a location is one of our biggest customers. We fly lots of cargo and fuel to them and bring their garbage back to McMurdo, where they freeze the waste.

"When we receive a tasking to fly a daytime mission to the South Pole, we look through details of the cargo we're carrying, study the route and take note of the South Pole weather forecasts. We then calculate how much cargo and fuel we can take to the pole and maximise how much fuel we can give them. Typically, we take off from McMurdo at our 155,000lb maximum weight, which requires us to use the entire ski way. As an example, if we carry 15,000lb of cargo and give the station 8,000lb of fuel, for our return flight we must calculate the minimum amount of fuel required to get back to McMurdo safely, which is dependent on the forecasted weather.

"One interesting fact is that Antarctica is about the size of North America, which has about 28,000 weather forecasting stations, the data from which builds a weather model for the entire nation. Antarctica has 28 stations, so the weather picture can be challenging to get right, using a bunch of different sources to

Right: **Crew from the 109th Airlift Wing perform maintenance on an LC-130 engine at Kangerlussuaq Airport Greenland.**
US Air National Guard/SSgt Madison Scaringe

Below: **An LC-130 being prepped for a mission at McMurdo Station, Antarctica.**
US Air National Guard/Major Shay Price

create the model. The weather is very dynamic and changing all the time, so battling it is our biggest challenge. You can take off and, an hour later, a blizzard will have rolled in behind you. We try our best to make sure that doesn't happen by looking at satellite imagery and historical data and using other sources of information. Our weather shop is the first stop on our way to the briefing, to get a picture of how things are looking.

"When we land at McMurdo, we usually keep the aircraft engines running. If we shut them down, we put the bird to bed and, the next morning, maintenance uses heaters to get the aircraft's systems preheated to help start the engines. Once we fly to a camp, the engines are constantly running until we get back to McMurdo, to keep the fluids from freezing.

"Another crucial aspect is to plan our missions so that we never have to take gas. Our goal is always to give gas to the out camps. We spend a lot of time planning to make sure we always have options and places to come back to. If we go to the South Pole to deliver cargo and the weather deteriorates back at McMurdo when we are on the ice, we always have enough fuel to shoot multiple approaches, in the hope that the weather during one of those approaches gets high enough that we've got the visibility to land.

"There are plenty of times when such a scenario doesn't happen. The weather deteriorates and we cannot get through to land, but we'll have enough gas to get back to McMurdo. Things get critical when we return to McMurdo and the weather deteriorates and we don't have an alternative airfield. In 2023, we had a crew that was preparing to take-off from the South Pole when the weather got poor. We had to hold the crew at the South Pole, and they spent the night there until the weather improved. Most of

Above: **An airman refuels an LC-130 while it is loaded with cargo at McMurdo Station for delivery to a research station in Antarctica.** US Air National Guard/Major Shay Price

Below: **An LC-130 is prepared for a mission at McMurdo Station, Antarctica.** US Air National Guard/Major Shay Price

our flight engineers have an extensive background in maintenance and can get the bird going in the morning without having maintenance airmen with them.

"If were at an outfield with the weather closing in for an unknown period, our options depend on the weather picture: how long we're going to be waiting and how much fuel we're going to burn while waiting. As a crew, we weigh up all those risks and bounce ideas off each other, drawing on the experience of the flight engineer, the pilots, loadmaster and navigator.

"The flight from Christchurch to McMurdo lasts between eight and nine hours. Wind conditions are a critical factor. About halfway we reach the point of safe return, where we have enough fuel to turn around and go back to Christchurch. We call McMurdo to get an update on the weather, which must be above certain minimums before we're legally allowed to continue. If you're past the point of safe

PROJECT ICEPOD

Project IcePod was conducted by Columbia University's Lamont Doherty Earth Observatory to map the Arctic and Antarctic. The project lasted three years and finished in the fall of 2017.

It involved flying an LC-130 equipped with a boom mounted to the floor and hooked into the D rings in the parachute doorway on the left-hand side of the plane. The parachute door was replaced by a viewing door, which allowed the whole cabin to be pressurised and kept warm. The door stayed up and the boom was fitted with an IcePod imaging system that extended out.

The IcePod is a modular, integrated, ice imaging system that can measure surface elevation, ice thickness and structure in high resolution from the surface to the bed. The system is enclosed in a Common Science Support Pod (the boom), mounted to the rear troop door of an LC-130. The instruments can collect an array of measurements during both routine and targeted missions across Antarctica and Greenland.

return and the weather turns bad, we have no options. In such a situation, we have a procedure that involves using an area off the departure end of one of the ski ways called the emergency white out area, where there's nothing to impact. We burn down our fuel, set a certain pitch in power and hold it until the aircraft performs a controlled crash. It takes the whole crew working together to execute a successful outcome."

Training

Landing on ski ways is a specific skill, the training for which can only be completed on the ice. There are no simulator profiles available for much of the ski training, as Lieutenant Colonel Dickerson explained: "In Antarctica, one limiting factor is the narrow window available in which to train new pilots, but we have a unique ability to tutor our pilots while we're conducting operational missions. For example, a qualified ski instructor pilot can fly an operational mission with a brand-new co-pilot fresh from training at Little Rock. The new co-pilot is qualified to fly the C-130 and are aware of the differences between the C-130 and LC-130. They work through a syllabus to learn the ski mission and fly it for real on operational missions with cargo and scientists onboard.

"Each year we have five opportunities during our summer in Greenland and a four-month season on the ice in Antarctica. That amounts to six months of the year when we can execute our ski mission on the snow and ice. In Greenland we operate from Kangerlussuaq Airport, formerly Sondrestrom Air Base, located at the base of the ice cap near Sondrestrom fjord. We take off from Kangerlussuaq's paved runway, immediately climb and within five minutes we're over the top of the Greenland ice cap. The flight to the Raven camp is 40 minutes. Raven is a ski way, and its sole purpose is to train our pilots

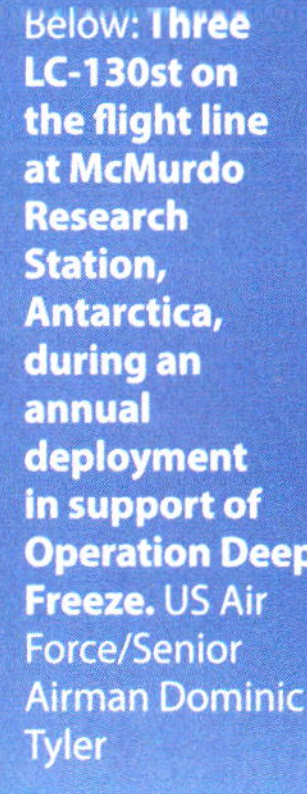

Below: **Three LC-130st on the flight line at McMurdo Research Station, Antarctica, during an annual deployment in support of Operation Deep Freeze.** US Air Force/Senior Airman Dominic Tyler

to complete ski take-offs and landings and for our navigators to complete airborne radar approaches. It's an old Distant Early Warning radar site.

"The nature of this mission means you've only got half the amount of time to learn. It takes seven years to qualify as an aircraft commander, which seems like a long time, but when you're on the ice for such a short amount of that time, it's hard for somebody to get the firsthand experience required.

"We treat an ice take-off like a short field take-off for a smaller airplane. We raise the nose at 60 knots and accelerate until the plane flies off the runway. We take off at near stall speed, complete a flare and use aircraft attitude to get airborne."

Crew Chief and Loadmaster

Discussing the crew chief's role on the ice, senior airman Staff Sergeant Kyler Buyce

said: "You tend to get more hydraulic weeping in the cold environment, so you're battling more hydraulic leaks than in a normal warm environment. We must complete work/rest cycles and swap out for snow. When the aircraft is placed on jacks, it tends to settle into the snow, at which point we reseat the jacks. Prior to an engine start, we preheat the props and heat up the aircraft for about an hour, so the systems aren't cold soaked and there's not as much stress on our hydraulic systems, avionics and electrical equipment.

"The JATO bottles undergo periodic inspections and NDI to search for cracks. The bottles are installed by our electricians. There are three pin-points with moveable latches, the bottle slides into a cam and is locked, after which the igniters are installed.

"While deployed to Antarctica, an LC-130 crew chief must be prepared to be outside in the cold throughout

12-hour workdays. We use heater carts in the immediate area of where we're conducting maintenance. We wear thin mechanics' gloves when dexterity is required and wear heavier duty winter gloves at other times. Our clothing keeps us warm down to -40°F, and we can warm-up in shacks and vehicles. Emergency cold weather gear is always stowed on the airplane.

"Our loadmasters work in pretty much the same way as a loadmaster on a standard C-130, with a couple of additional duties when they're on the ice. They load cargo placed on sleds, but don't have K-loaders to lift the cargo up and down. Instead, the loadmaster kneels the aircraft by dipping the front or the back, to align the plane with the loading sled."

Ski Way Flagging

Landing on ice is a unique procedure, according to Major Clark: "Runways or ski ways are marked with flags with metal woven into them to allow our radar to get a strong return, which allows the navigator to paint the ski way and talk the pilots down for landing. We also flag the ends of the ski way and position lead-in flags at two miles out, which helps to get us lined up and indicate how far out we are from the ski way.

"Because ski ways move, we have different cardinal headings each year. Every year the flagging is checked and certified on the ground by the installation team and the aircrew. Until the flags are certified, we typically use increased weather minimums to get into a facility.

"It's a very challenging mission, the weather and a lack of material handling equipment requires us to be expeditionary and we must solve a lot of problems ourselves. People we've taken on missions are surprised when they see the conditions we land and take off in. Take-offs are so different to those experienced on an airliner."

SUBSCRIBE TODAY!

Airforces Monthly is devoted to modern military aircraft and their air arms.

/collections/subscriptions

Free 2nd class P&P on BFPO orders. Overseas charges apply.

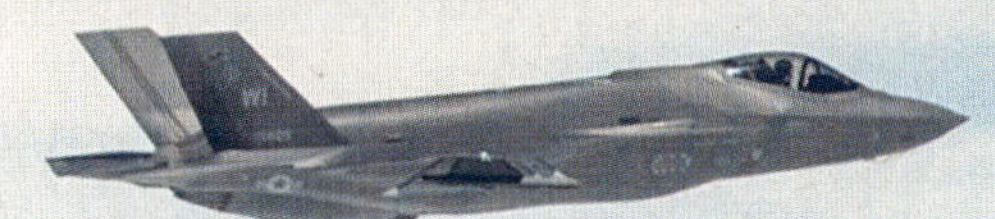

BADGER AIR MILITIA

Wisconsin ANG's 115th Fighter Wing is the second unit to operate the F-35A Lightning II for worldwide operations

COLONEL BEN GERDS, commander of the 115th Fighter Wing from the Wisconsin Air National Guard, started his career as a weapons systems specialist. He is an experienced fighter pilot with more than 2,000 hours on the F-16, who has now transitioned to the F-35A. Hi colleague, Colonel Statz, has worked as an aircraft maintainer throughout his career and now serves as deputy commander of the 115th FW. In a joint interview, they provided their respective overviews of the 115th's F-35A alert mission from Truax Field near Madison, Wisconsin.

Discussing the F-35A, Gerds said: "A decision was made, and the appropriate documents were signed for the wing's transition with the 36-month conversion set for October 2022 to October 2025. We started the process by identifying what construction projects were required to support the F-35 assignment and also started planning the divestment of our F-16 aircraft. We worked with National Guard Bureau to formulate a plan for where our F-16 aircraft would be re-assigned.

"We started divesting F-16s and the associated equipment to different units around the country in October 2022. Concurrently, we identified an initial core cadre of maintainers to train on the F-35. That group of people were sent to active-duty F-35 bases and Vermont Air National Guard's 158th Fighter Wing at Burlington for 24 months of training. They returned to Madison to work and train on F-35 aircraft assigned to the 115th FW, the first of which arrived in late April 2023. We followed a similar process for training some of our pilots.

"Initially, we flew a small turn pattern for the pilots and slowly increased the daily schedule as our maintainers became more proficient. Today, we're flying a fuller pattern with a complete complement of pilots and maintainers. The wing is close to completing its conversion, at which point we will be ready for the homeland defence mission at Madison and worldwide deployment."

How did that process impact the pilots and maintainers? Colonel Statz said: "One beneficial aspect of our transition was the ability to maintain the same manning document we had for the F-16, so we didn't have to downsize, but we did have to divest six different maintenance shops. In trying to meet the force management plan, we had to manage people's career plans across the board.

"We also had the benefit of supporting the alert mission, which is being maintained during our transition period by the F-16C-equipped 148th Fighter Wing from Duluth, so some of our personnel were able to stay on just to support that. For some of those people and others who opted to retire, the wing helped them to find other jobs outside the organisation.

"Many maintainers cross-trained to a different shop, for example, from the engine or hydraulic shops to crew chiefs or from the electrical shop to avionics. For some who were resident experts in their career field on the F-16, it was a little uncomfortable when given a brand-new system and asked to figure it out. About 52 active-duty airmen with F-35 experience assigned to the

378th Fighter Squadron, our total force squadron, to instruct our maintainers about the complexity of the F-35 and the new mission. That was extremely helpful through transition."

Discussing the same transitional issue faced by pilots, Colonel Gerds explained that he was the 176th Fighter Squadron commander when the transition started: "I spoke with each pilot about their desire to transition from the F-16 to the F-35 and their commitment to work through the entire process. For those who were at the end of their career, transition didn't make sense, and they elected to retire. Several pilots who were at the mid-point of their flying career and wanted to transition were asked to give a multi-year commitment. We also had to hire new pilots to fill our ranks, which included former US Navy F/A-18 Hornet and F-35C pilots and a large contingent of former active-duty USAF pilots. Another highly beneficial aspect of the total force integration programme with the 378th Fighter Squadron was gained from having four active-duty F-35 pilots, including

Above: **F-35 Lightning II aircraft assigned to the 115th Fighter Wing refuelling from a KC-135R Stratotanker assigned to the 128th ARW at Milwaukee International Airport during the delivery flight to Truax Field on April 25, 2023.** US Air National Guard/SSgt Cameron Lewis

one F-35 weapons officer, and about 40 active-duty maintenance folks integrated into our unit."

Construction Work

As part of the transition, the 115th FW had 20 F-35-specific projects, plus two additional military construction projects running at the same time, with a combined worth of over $160 million. Colonel Statz explained: "It's significant for our installation to receive that level of improvements. It solidified the importance of our installation to the USAF, but also solidified our mission, no matter what the platform. To the best of my knowledge, our base was the first to get its simulator facility up and running before the first aircraft arrived. The simulators allowed our pilots and those from other units to maintain some currency during the period when the wing's brand-new TR-3 aircraft remained at Fort Worth due to software certification issues. Simulators are an important part of the ready aircrew programme, which requires pilots to maintain currency and also help

alleviate changes that had to be made to individual pilots training plans.

"We got a lot of support from the National Guard Bureau to increase our contracting and civil engineering capacity for the workflow that went ahead during our transition period – we received $160 million's worth of work in three years. Outside of transition we may receive $2.5 million, so a significant annual increase."

Homeland Defence

At the end of its transition on September 30, 2025, and the start of the new fiscal year for 2026 on October 1, the 115th FW must be ready to hold the 24/7 alert in support of the homeland defence mission under Operation Noble Eagle.

Discussing the preparations underway to prepare for that tasking, Colonel Statz said: "We're working through the techniques, tactics and procedures of the alert mission and training to prepare for the objective date. We will be the first F-35 wing in the entire USAF to stand the alert mission. [Operation Noble Eagle is run by the 1st Air Force based at

Above: **F-35 Lightning II aircraft assigned to the 115th FW perform aerial refuelling from a KC-135R assigned to the 128th ARW at Milwaukee.** US Air National Guard/SSgt Cameron Lewis

Tyndall Air Force Base, Florida, for which all alerts across the US are held by ANG fighter wings].

"We're also working towards the end of our conversion, when we'll report our readiness to complete our wartime tasking, making sure that we have all the required equipment for our unit tasking codes (UTCs), bringing on additional pilots and maintainers to make sure we complete all the manning document requirements and have what we need as one of the few ANG deployable combat wings.

"In addition to those requirements, we've gained the suppression of enemy air defences role with the F-35, for which we've spent a lot of time studying and becoming proficient to execute. I think it's a bread-and-butter role of the F-35."

God Bless the Maintainers

Leading a group of enlisted airmen who work for the 115th Maintenance Group is the job of Chief Master Sergeant Jared Calhoun, who is the maintenance group senior enlisted leader. Calhoun

has served with the 115th FW has a comprehensive level of maintenance experience, much of it with F-16Cs. Airmen under his watch faced a series of challenges during the wing's transition to the F-35A. The greatest was divesting the wing's F-16C aircraft in conjunction with the construction of new and remodelled aircraft facilities, made tougher by the weather in Wisconsin, space limitations and conducting flight operations without interruption until Minnesota ANG 's F16-equipped 148th Fighter Wing took responsibility for the alert. Aircraft divestment lasted until March 2023.

Recalling the training effort, Calhoun said: "During 2020 and 2021, we sent two groups of personnel for initial F-35 training at various operating bases. They returned here after 24 and 12 months away. In May 2023, 150 people started training at our home station after the first aircraft arrived at Truax Field. Because weapons troops are not allowed to load on two different aircraft types without a waiver, a small group of them are still working on F-16s from the 148th Fighter Wing on the alert mission.

"In February 2023, we accepted and inducted F-35 support equipment to our inventory, a process which was challenged by a shortage of storage space for keeping the equipment under cover. After the first F-35s arrived here in April 23, we started flying regular F-35 sorties in May and ramped that effort up during the summer. The ramp-up was made possible by the growing number of our maintainers who had qualified on the new aircraft. Once we had our near-full complement of aircraft, we were able to follow an eight-turn-four flight schedule."

During the suspension of F-35 aircraft deliveries invoked by the F-35 Joint Program Office, the 115th FW was short of aircraft at a time when 150 or more of its maintenance airmen were qualified on the type, which slowed their training progression. Maintainers assigned to the 115th Maintenance Squadron continue to train to get fully certified on the aircraft.

Approximately 20% of the crew working for the maintenance squadron and group opted to retire rather than convert to the F-35. Calhoun explained:

that those limitations will be addressed in the future.

"Last year [2024], we went to Tyndall Air Force Base on our first TDY with the F-35 for Combat Archer, a weapon system evaluation programme run by Air Combat Command. The programme is designed to evaluate all maintenance actions required to build, handle, load and shoot missiles, some of them live. We had zero deficiencies, which is unheard of. In January, we deployed six aircraft to Savannah ANG Base in Georgia for a joint exercise called Century Savannah. In addition to flying our aircraft from Savannah, we also launched four-ships from Truax Field on over-the-horizon missions to participate in the exercise, fight and return then return to Madison, all with tanker support. The over-the-horizon missions were good preparation for executing agile combat employment (ACE) operations. We've already exercised ACE during a combat readiness inspection in August 2024, when we operated from two different locations and completed scenario-based events while trying to understand our abilities and limitations associated with to the computerised nature of

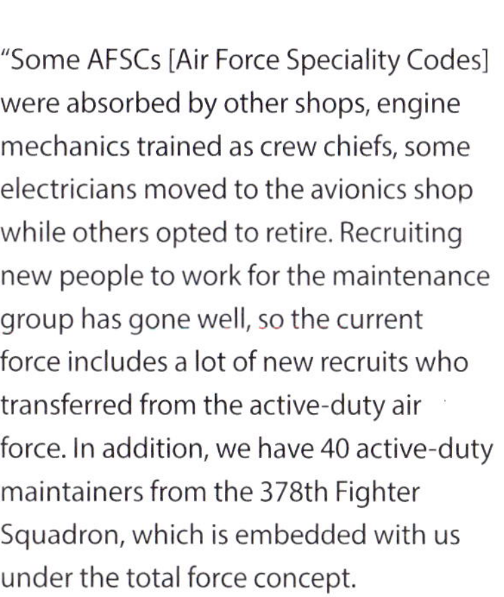

"Some AFSCs [Air Force Speciality Codes] were absorbed by other shops, engine mechanics trained as crew chiefs, some electricians moved to the avionics shop while others opted to retire. Recruiting new people to work for the maintenance group has gone well, so the current force includes a lot of new recruits who transferred from the active-duty air force. In addition, we have 40 active-duty maintainers from the 378th Fighter Squadron, which is embedded with us under the total force concept.

"Our avionics folks were challenged by a variety of complex issues. That said, their experience with the F-35 has accelerated beyond my expectation for this stage of the transition. We are still using ALIS [the Autonomic Logistics Information System, used for tracking and checking the maintenance status of each aircraft and recording all maintenance activity completed on an individual airframe] and we've embraced the system. Our maintainers have adapted to it a lot better than expected. It has its limitations on certain things, but across the enterprise the expectation is

Below: **A KC-135R Stratotanker assigned to the 128th ARW refuels an F-35A Lightning II aircraft assigned to the 115th Fighter Wing.** US Air National Guard/SSgt Anya Hanson

the jet. For example, learning how to move for a TDY in conjunction with the technical representatives, who are civilian contractors who currently need to deploy with the aircraft to manage ALIS to support flight ops and maintenance."

Fighter Squadron

Wisconsin ANG's 115th Fighter Wing has three groups assigned: maintenance, medical and operations. The 115th Operations Group has three squadron, of which the flying component is the 176th Fighter Squadron. Its current commander is Lieutenant Colonel Mike Koob, an experienced F-16 pilot and F-35 weapons officer.

Discussing the transition from the fighter squadron perspective, Koob said: "When you transition to such a complex, state-of-the-art aircraft – and you're doing it with a part time force, especially on the maintenance side – there's some challenges, but those are common to every unit that transitions to the F-35.

"After 9/11, the ANG became an operational force that deployed its fighter wings and others on the same air expeditionary force cycle, as the active duty which changed the identity of the guard. Here in Wisconsin, we went from being a strategic reserve to a full-time force. Post-9/11, the 115th FW picked up Operation Noble Eagle, the homeland defence mission. We've maintained the alert mission since 2001, but during our transition the alert is maintained by Minnesota ANG's 148th FW at Duluth. Some of their F-16s are here in Madison but, come this October, we will resume the homeland defence mission with the F-35s in Madison.

"Every pilot's transition from the F-16 to the F-35 has been unique. In my case, after taking the F-35 B-course and subsequent upgrades, I served with the 6th Weapons Squadron, the USAF Weapons School F-35 schoolhouse at Nellis Air Force Base, Nevada, learning how to become an F-35 weapons instructor. For all the pilots who transitioned to the F-35, it was a humbling experience to be a student once again, having previously flown thousands of hours in the F-16.

"The jet is incredibly easy to fly. Its systems and technologies reduce the pilot's workload. When flying the F-16, a lot of your energy goes into making the jet perform the way you want. When flying the F-35, so much of that is automated – auto throttle, auto pilot and sensor fusion which automatically shares data with the pilot such that the pilot must prioritise their role at any given time. The challenge in the F-35 is the sheer amount of information that's presented to you – so much data, so many details on your display – it's a level of situational awareness that you did not have in the F-16. Identifying and prioritising what they need from the information and what to execute makes the pilot's job one of battle management.

"When training a young wingman in the F-16 we spend much of the time maintaining visual formation. In the event the young wingman gets lost, it is hard for them to find you again, which resulted in us expending time to find the wingman. In the F-35, we rarely fly visual formations, but almost exclusively perform sensor formations, where my wingman is miles away from me. For the young wingman flying in their own battle management sphere, my responsibility as the flight lead is to tell them what to prioritise during each phase of the mission, whether its air-to-surface, SEAD, escort or air-to-air. It's a very different mentality, and it's challenging to get used to how the F-35 operates, even for experienced pilots.

TR-2 and TR-3

With a few F-35s configured to Technical Refresh 2 (TR-2) standard and the propensity of jets configured in the latest TR-3 standard, the 115th FW operates the F-35 with slight differences between

Below: **An F-35A Lightning II aircraft taking off from Tyndall Air force Base, Florida, during Exercise Combat Archer.** US Air National Guard/ SSgt Anya Hanson

Above: **Aircraft maintenance specialists with Wisconsin Air National Guard's 115th Fighter Wing, raise a grounding rod during Combat Archer at Tyndall Air force Base, Florida, on February 13, 2024.** US Air National Guard/SSgt Anya Hanson

the two. Koob explained: "The F-35's first flight was on December 15, 2006. A lot of the hardware installed in the original F-35s is already very dated – the defence acquisition process from product definition to customer delivery is already more than ten years old and obsolete. Decisions were made to conduct sequential technical refreshes to the F-35 designated TR-1, TR-2, and the current TR-3. Each one was cut into production at a specific airframe.

"TR-3 standard aircraft have numerous hardware changes and an upgraded integrated core processor. The downside of that and some dysfunction with the aircraft's operating software means we don't currently have a fully functional software suite installed in the jets. Our TR-3 jets were placed in storage at Fort Worth for several months, until the F-35 Joint Program Office approved them for flight training operations.

"Fortunately, we've not encountered any vehicle systems or safety of flight issues associated directly with TR-3, but there are some kinks in the current software load which require us to follow workaround procedures. Once the software catches up, we'll have very capable jets with no pending requirement for a multi-month visit to the depot for expensive upgrades to TR-3 configuration. Operating a fleet comprising TR-2 and TR-3 aircraft presents no real hardships, just minor issues. The TR-3 jets have more issues to overcome, which in the short-term may affect us when we resume our alert on October 1. We'll instead use our TR-2 jets for the alert. When we went to Savannah for Century South 2025, we had less than 5% of planned sorties suffer ground aborts, but the aircraft should be serviceable since they're brand-new.

"From a squadron commander's perspective, the best thing about the F-35 is the ability to fly any mission at any time without the need for our maintainers to configure the aircraft for a specific mission set. On any day we can train to any mission the F-35 is capable of performing, so on a basic fighter manoeuvring (BFM) training day, if the weather doesn't allow BFM to be flown, I can flip into air-to-surface training, climb above the weather and use the radar's multi-function array to generate synthetic aperture maps, target designate and simulate dropping bombs through the weather, a capability that's also beneficial to our pilot upgrade training programmes."

Combat Archer and Century South

When Koob led the deployment to Tyndall Air Force Base, Florida for Combat Archer, it was the wing's first movement of F-35s since the transition period started. This involved taking new

Right: **A tactical aircraft maintenance specialist assigned to the 378th Fighter Squadron services an F-35A during Exercise Sentry F-35 25-1 at the Air Dominance Center at F-35 Air National Guard Base, Georgia.** US Air National Guard/MSgt Mary Greenwood

equipment on the road that airmen were still getting familiar with.

Koob said: "Combat Archer is Air Combat Command's air-to-air weapon systems evaluation programme. It's a graded event in which inspectors evaluate 35 areas, including weapon handling, weapon loading and weapon firing. It was the squadron's first time firing missiles with the F-35, and we received zero discrepancies. The mix of missiles fired included a couple of AIM-9 Sidewinders and more AIM-120 AMRAAMs. None of the missiles fired were fitted with a warhead, yet several caused fireballs when they hit the drone target, causing the drone to splash down in the Gulf of Mexico."

The squadron's second TDY took place in January 2025 to Savannah Air National Guard Base for participation in Exercise Century South 25-1. The airspace available to players in the exercise is rated by pilots as phenomenal, starting just 15 miles off the Atlantic coast and extending from sea level to 60,000ft, with supersonic flight permitted. Describing the exercise, Koon said: "The biggest learning experience for our pilots was integration with F-22 Raptors from the 71st Fighter Squadron at Langley Air Force Base, Virginia. Any chance we get to integrate with F-22s is beneficial because the two types complement each other

Left: **F-35A 20-5621/WI painted with tail markings for the 115th Operations Group.** US Air National Guard/ MSgt Mary Greenwood

exceptionally well and make a formidable force element. We had F-22s performing offensive counter air utilising the aircraft's air-to-air prowess, while we practiced our F-35's air-to-surface capabilities over land."

Chief Calhoun added: "We flew two over-the-horizon missions from Madison as a test of our pilots to fly long-range missions and execute distributed mission planning. We sent mission planning information from Savannah to the pilots at Madison and conducted a brief via a secure video conference system. The pilots who flew from Madison had to manage their fuel loads, rendezvous with tankers, arrive in the airspace on time, execute the mission and return home. It was a good opportunity for some of our flight leads to participate in long-range missions, which lasted for six-and-a-half hours.

"Participation in Century South allowed us to determine how we're performing as a fighter squadron and gave a chance for us to determine our overall understanding of the tactics used to integrate with other aircraft types, as we did in Century Savannah. The exercise was well timed as we work toward the completion of our transition period."

Final Words

Summing up their experience, Gerds said: "Our selection for the F-35 was based, in part, on the symbiotic partnership we have between the KC-135R wing at Milwaukee and the Combat Readiness Training Center at Volk Field and its extensive airspace. Our F-35s connect all the assets and their capabilities, which help us bring other assets from other services together for large force exercises and day-to-day training opportunities in Wisconsin. We've conducted agile combat employment at Volk Field and at Alpena, Michigan."

F-35A 22-5697/WI from the 115th Fighter Wing at the Air Dominance Center at F-35 Air National Guard Base, Georgia. US Air National Guard/MSgt Mary Greenwood

RED HAWKS

Based at Portland International Airport, Oregon Air National Guard's 142nd Wing is the first operational unit for the F-15EX Eagle II

COLONEL DANIEL MCALLISTER is the commander of the 142nd Maintenance Group (MXG) based at Portland, a post he's held since December 2024. His responsibilities are many but primarily involve overseeing the maintenance of a fleet of fighters comprising legacy F-15C Eagles and brand-new F-15EX Eagle IIs.

The 142nd MXG comprises the 142nd Maintenance Squadron (MXS), the 142nd Aircraft Maintenance Squadron (AMXS) and the 142nd Maintenance Operations Flight, with nearly 400 personnel assigned across the MXG.

Maintenance

Col McAllister is tasked with keeping the fleet of legacy F-15C Eagles combat-ready for potential deployment and spinning up maintenance procedures and activities as a major part of the wing's ongoing transition to the F-15EX.

Discussing the time and effort given to maintaining the F-15C fleet, McAllister said: "Availability of spare parts is a challenge, but it's largely overcome by the level of experience and expertise of this cadre of maintainers, some of whom have 30-plus years of service with the wing."

Concurrently managing two different variants of the F-15 has required effective planning to train an initial group of people qualified to work on the F-15EX and, as F-15C aircraft are divested and EX-models are delivered to the wing, more maintenance personnel will be qualified on the EX until the 142nd Operations Group is fully equipped with the new type.

Most of the 142nd's fleet of F-15C Eagles were previously assigned to the active-duty air force, many from the 18th Wing based at Kadena Air Base, Okinawa, Japan. Explaining what happens when new aircraft are delivered to the wing, McAllister said: "Whenever we accept an aircraft from another unit, it undergoes an inspection to check its condition, the factor that drives the length of that process. Despite the age of our aircraft [procured between Fiscal Years 1984 and 1986] most underwent depot level maintenance relatively recently, so they're in good condition after their teardown at the Warner Robins Air Logistics Complex in Georgia.

"Our aircraft are maintained in accordance with the air force phased inspection process, with each inspection

Below: **F-15EX Eagle II 20-008 assigned to the 142nd Wing takes off from Portland Air National Guard Base, Oregon, on July 12, 2024, officially unveiling the aircraft to the public. The 142nd Wing had welcomed its first F-15EX on June 5.** US Air National Guard/ SSgt Nichole Sanchez

conducted after the airframe has flown a specified number of flight hours since its previous inspection. The aircraft is taken out of the flying schedule so a deep-dive inspection can take place to make sure everything is compliant, and we address problems found on the jet.

"F-15C aircraft are at the end of their service lives, so the parts and components that fail are those that we expect to break on a 40-year-old aircraft. Thankfully, our maintainers have worked on these airplanes for so long that they can figure out the problem because they've seen the issue pop up many times.

"To train our maintainers on the F-15EX, we sent some to Boeing in St Louis and others to Eglin Air Force Base. Those that went to Eglin leveraged the experience of the maintainers working on the F-15EX aircraft assigned to the two test wings based there. Beyond that training and largely because we're the first operational unit to get the F-15EX, we're figuring out things that weren't discovered in flight test at Eglin or by Boeing at St Louis. Our maintainers are finding new and unforeseen issues on the EX, and they're devising solutions. In many ways, we're writing the book for how to field this airplane and setting the standard for

the other units that will transition to the EX after us, under the oversight of Air Combat Command, the National Guard Bureau and Boeing.

"There are many possibilities in terms of how the US Air Force wants to use F-15EX for which we're awaiting guidance, but we anticipate that we're going to be asked to do more. Additional mission sets will affect the 142nd Munitions Flight in terms of what weapons it would load on the airplane, and potentially some of our avionics folks."

Operations Group

The 142nd Wing, currently operating F-15C and F-15EX fighters, has one of two Air National Guard (ANG) special tactics squadrons, comprising pararescuemen and combat controllers with a unique capability for precision fires and global strikes, and an air control squadron that for now operates a large radar facility on the coast of Oregon but is converting to the cyber operations role. Transitioning to a potentially multi-role mission set with the F-15EX touches so many different domains, air-to-air, air-to-ground, space and cyber, so all the capabilities will be part of the future air power.

Providing insight to the wing's current activities, the 142nd Operations Group

commander, Lieutenant Colonel Jeffrey Yeates, said: "Since we received the first two Lot1B F-15EX aircraft in June 2024, we've flown the aircraft with an initial cadre of instructors who are validating a training syllabus before we spin up as the lead operational EX unit. We have the only two F-15EX simulators, which enable us to develop syllabus academics and a training plan and validate them before the syllabus events are flown.

"Our two EX aircraft have each been flying two to three times a week, somewhat constrained by our small group of instructors who have limited availability to plan and fly the syllabus missions and by our maintainers who are kept busy learning the new aircraft.

"We expect to receive our third airplane in March, after which we expect to realise Boeing's delivery rate of one to two aircraft per month to complete our F-15EX transition in Fiscal Year 2024. One current challenge is identifying who gets converted over to the F-15EX, which we're likely to mitigate by qualifying our experienced pilots and instructors in both the F-15C and the F-15EX. For the next six months were working on how we spin up the squadron and create what will amount to a one-way door for our less experienced F-15C pilots to transition to the F-15EX.

Once they complete their conversion, that's the only variant they will fly.

"In terms of learning to operate the F-15EX, there is commonality in the HOTAS [hands on throttle-and-stick, the concept of placing buttons and switches on the throttle lever and flight control stick], in the way information is presented to the pilot and in the way the aircraft flies, such that you can effectively and quickly put somebody into the air. But to truly capitalise on the jet's additional capabilities is a bigger challenge that requires more work and time to train up a pilot to get them to the required level of proficiency.

"For our experienced pilots, maintaining currency in both variants is the challenge, which is particularly acute for us because we stand on alert for Operation Noble Eagle in support of NORAD and NORTHCOM for the defence of North America in co-operation with Canada. We have a 24/7 alert facility here at Portland, so planning for when we put the F-15EX on alert as a fielded weapon system ready to launch, and how we train our pilots to be ready for the alert mission, are primary objectives. The inflection point between F-15C and F-15EX is still to be determined, but we anticipate the F-15EX will be put on alert ready to scramble after an airborne threat, later this year."

Given the 142nd Wing is equipped with two F-15EX simulators, there is a good chance the wing will conduct pilot conversions for other wings in addition to its own. Explaining the situation, Yeates said: "We sent our initial cadre of pilots to Eglin, where they received academics and training flights with the two F-15EX test squadron. They returned to Portland to train the next group of instructors here. The 44th and 67th Fighter Squadrons assigned to the 18th Wing at Kadena will spin up after us. As of right now, Kadena does not have simulators for the F-15EX so pilots and maintainers will train here. We have a large contingent of Kadena-based maintainers here at Portland for the next couple of months to get their initial hands-on training with the F-15EX. We anticipate that continuing for the next year or so as Boeing delivers Kadena jets to Portland to stage before they ferry to Kadena. Our wing's instructors and experienced pilots will train Kadena pilots and leverage the

Above: **F-15C Eagle 78-483 assigned to the 123rd Fighter Squadron, Oregon ANG, taxis at the Air Dominance Center in Savannah, Georgia, during Sentry Savannah in 2021.** US Army National Guard/Captain Bryant Wine

F-15EX Eagle II 20-007 taxis at Boeing's delivery centre at St Louis on its delivery flight to Portland ANG base, Oregon. The aircraft is painted with full colour tail markings, including a Red Hawk motif. *Boeing*

Pilots conducted dissimilar air combat training, ground-controlled interception and aerial refuelling.

Yeates explained: "Oregon's state partnership programme is with Bangladesh and Vietnam. Neither nation presents opportunities to send airplanes in co-operative exercises due to strategic concerns. Washington state, on the other hand, is partnered with Thailand, which operates F-16 and Gripen fighters so it was decided we would conduct a co-operative state partnership programme leveraging the Washington Air National Guard's KC-135s with our F-15Cs. The two wings deployed to Korat and flew with Royal Thai Air Force F-16s and Gripens. The deployment presented some challenges, including aircraft maintenance problems, during the transit across the Pacific and a lack of ability to get all the aircraft to and from Korat.

"The programme creates partnerships into areas of the world that are difficult to access, often by the DoD. But it does create problems because it is an ad hoc Air National Guard programme, and we don't always have the support aircraft required."

simulators for that task – it will take time to install simulators at Kadena because of the construction required."

The 142nd Wing's current taskings are above and beyond its core air dominance mission and its ability to carry that workload is based, according to Yeates "on the amount of experience in Air National Guard wings". He said: "At any given time, we have multiple instructor pilots and weapons officers from the US Air Force Weapons School and the US Navy TOPGUN Fighter Weapons School in our squadron, far more than any active-duty squadron I've been assigned to during my career. For example, in a recent meeting, we had 14 instructor pilots in attendance."

As the first F-15EX-equipped wing, Yeates and his colleagues are pathfinders in developing basic aircraft procedures for entry into the F-15EX 3-1 manual, which has not yet been developed. This work covers tactics as straightforward as how to do instrument trail procedures in adverse weather to get to the airspace, or what power settings to use for tactical execution where the pilot no longer has the legacy AWR-56C radar warning receiver but has the brand-new Eagle Passive Active Warning Survivability System – and how to use that defensively. All such tactics are currently being written and worked on at the Portland-based wing.

Exercise Participation

In September 2023, airmen from Washington ANG's KC-135R-equipped 141st Air Refueling Wing and Oregon ANG's 142nd Wing participated in the first-ever Enduring Partners engagement with the Royal Thai Air Force at Korat air base in Thailand.

The exercise was a National Guard-sponsored state partnership programme engagement aimed at improving combat readiness and combined and joint interoperability between participants while enhancing strong defence relations between the Washington ANG and Thailand.

The 142nd Wing deployed five F-15Cs supported by two 141st ARW KC-135Rs.

Above: **A weapons loader assigned to the 142nd Maintenance Group handles a live AIM-120 AMRAAN missile at Langley Air Force Base, Virginia, at the alert facility under Operation Noble Eagle.** US Air National Guard/SSgt Sean Campbell

Right: **Armament airmen assigned to the 142nd Aircraft Maintenance Squadron load a CATM-120 dummy missile at Portland ANG base.** US Air National Guard/SSgt Sean Campbell

Right: **F-15C 78-473 assigned to the 142nd Wing at the Air Dominance Center at Savannah, Georgia, during Century Savannah, the ANG's largest air-to-air, fourth and fifth-generation integration exercise.** US Army National Guard/Captain Bryant Wine

Lt Col Yeates added: "Our weapons officers and the fighter squadron commander have started developing a three-year training plan for the wing that integrates all our capabilities. We're looking to participate in a Combat Archer Weapons System Evaluation Program [WSEP] and Exercise Red Flag in 2026 followed by an advanced Combat Hammer WSEP in 2027. The F-15EX aircraft has tremendous capability and we at the 142nd Wing hope the air force procures more to increase our combat capability."

Weapons Evaluation

The 53rd Weapons Evaluation Group [WEG], a tenant organisation, based at Tyndall Air Force Base, Florida, is a component of Air Combat Command's 53rd Wing based at Eglin Air Force Base, also in Florida.

The group runs Combat Archer, Air Combat Command's air-to-air Weapons System Evaluation Program, which exercises and evaluates the system's capability of combat-coded fighter squadrons. Hosted at Tyndall by the

Above: **Pilots in F-15EX 20-008 under tow at Boeing's St Louis facility on June 5, 2024, prior to its delivery flight to the 142nd Wing at Portland.** Aaron Perkins, Oregon Military Department Public Affairs

83rd Fighter Weapons Squadron, personnel verify weapon system performance, determine reliability, evaluate capability and limitations, identify deficiencies, recommend corrective action and maintain combat air force-wide data. Additionally, the squadron investigates missile envelopes and evaluates capabilities and limitations to determine future firing requirements.

The 82nd Aerial Targets Squadron, at Tyndall, operates the US Department of Defense's only full-scale aerial target programme, with an inventory of approximately 80 modified QF-16 aircraft for this purpose. It also provides BQM-34 and BQM-167 subscale aerial targets in support of Combat Archer.

Discussing the 142nd Wing's participation in Combat Archer, Col McAllister said: "Our last visit to Tyndall for Combat Archer was in 2022. It's an important programme to be a part of, because it provides a lot of our training. Squadron pilots get to shoot a missile and see the weapon come off the airplane, and our maintainers get to load the missiles, which are both important skill sets. Our maintainers, weapons crews, munitions folks and pilots need to gain that experience so if they go to combat it isn't the first time they've ever dealt with a live weapon."

Personnel from the 142nd Wing stand in front of an F-15C with Lieutenant General Michael Loh, Director, Air National Guard, on Korat Air Base Royal Kingdom of Thailand, during Enduring Partners 2023. US Air National Guard/Senior Airman Yuki Klein

LONE STAR
GUNFIGHTERS

Part of the Texas Air National Guard, the 149th Fighter Wing based at Lackland Air Force Base near San Antonio continues to fly the F-16C Fighting Falcon as a formal training unit

LOCATED IN A corner of the sprawling Lackland Air Force Base (AFB) complex in Texas, the 149th Operations Group (OG) has a single assigned squadron, the 182nd Fighter Squadron, equipped with a fleet of Block 30 F-16C and F-16D fighters. The jets are used to train up to 40 active-duty Air National Guard (ANG) and Air Force Reserve pilots each year.

Explaining the wing's training effort, Lieutenant Colonel Caleb Cienski, chief of wing plans for the 149th Fighter Wing, said: "We run two six-month basic courses each year for pilots who have finished undergraduate pilot training and the introduction to fighter fundamentals syllabus. In an average year, we'll graduate around 20 pilots from the basic courses. An average class comprises between eight and ten pilots, including three guardsmen and two reservists plus those from the active duty. The mix is driven by aligning the completion date of a student's IFF syllabus with our course start date.

"During the summer, we typically run a transition course taken by pilots who are returning to flying duty after completion of a staff tour, or they're coming from another aircraft type and must learn the F-16 before joining a combat-coded squadron. We also run a senior officer course, which is appropriately named because it's for senior officers ranked O-6 and above. Such officers gain a basic qualification in the jet, [they] are unlikely to fly combat missions in the F-16, but fly locally at their assignment

base. Additionally, we run instructor pilot upgrades for other guard units."

The basic course is the same as one run by the active-duty 54th Fighter Group based at Holloman AFB, New Mexico, and Arizona ANG's 162nd Fighter Wing (FW) based at Tucson – same duration, same number of flights and simulators. However, the Tucson-based unit does instruct pilots from foreign military sale nations; the 182nd is US-only.

Experience

According to Lt Col Cienski, the 182nd Fighter Squadron (FS) is the most experienced F-16 squadron in the US Air Force (USAF), based on the average hours flown in the jet by each of its pilots, which is above 1,800 including 850 to 900 flown

as an instructor pilot: "The 149th FW is not combat-coded and does not deploy as a wing, but individual instructors volunteer to deploy with other Air National Guard or active-duty units.

"We have ten graduates of either the US Air Force Weapon School or TOPGUN in our instructor cadre, so highly experienced. Some have served with other units when deployed down range or at the unit's home station, to provide weapons officer experience.

"The main recruiting pool that we select from is that of active-duty instructor pilots who are finishing their service requirement and can separate from the active duty and join the guard. We have three, what we call guard babies, who were hired into a guard

Above: **An F-16 assigned to the 149th FW at Alpena Combat Readiness Training Center (CRTC), Michigan, during Exercise Northern Cactus, a joint training event staged at an austere environment to participate in a simulated deployment exercise.** US Air National Guard/ TSgt Derek Davis

unit, went to pilot training and then serve with the national guard. The other 20-plus pilots in our unit all served with the active duty prior to separating and joining the guard.

"We differ from a traditional guard unit by the number of full-time positions we are authorised, we're almost exclusively full-time because we have a continuous mission. Our staffing is completely inverted from a traditional guard unit, which generally has a smaller cadre of full-time positions who tend to 'keep the lights on' and complete all plans set up for drill weekends.

"Our instructor pilots follow the US Air Force Ready Aircrew Program [RAP], which sets out how many training sorties we need to fly to keep our combat edge. Because we fly in the basic course, some of the sorties can be termed vanilla for us; they provide good experience, build expertise of hands-on flying, leading the students, but it's not quite the same. Last summer we deployed to the Alpena Combat Readiness Training Center [CRTC] in Michigan and flew in a joint training exercise with F-35C aircraft operated by Marine Fighter Attack Squadron 311 [VMFA-311] in Exercise Northern Cactus. Morning missions were tasked as defensive counter-air exclusively for the instructor pilot cadre to get their RAP training.

"Most of our continuation training is undertaken on drill weekends when we give the students the weekend off so the

Left: **Avionics technicians assigned to the 149th FW conduct post flight maintenance and review of an F-16 during Northern Cactus at Alpena.** US Air National Guard/ TSgt Derek Davis

instructors can fly the required events to get re-qualified, specifically for doing low altitude training, or employing weapons on the nearby range."

Deployments

Explaining how the 149th FW's deploys in sync with its two B-courses each year, Cienski said: "Up until 2019, we ran one basic course a year. It started in August and graduated in May. Back then, we completed one two-week trip in the spring deploying to Luke or Tucson specifically to drop heavy weapons, which we can't drop on our ranges here in Texas. In 2020, we shortened the basic course, which enabled us to run two courses a year. Now we're working towards completing a single week deployment per course. It's good for all the support functions to be able to get off station to do their job at a different location and maintain their edge.

"That change trimmed the B-course a little bit, mostly to areas of the course that students got to and then moved on to the next syllabus event. In aggregate, the students can demonstrate proficiency as they move forward in the syllabus. So, we cut the number of sorties, to shorten the course, to increase production across the fighter enterprise.

"We've had many discussions on the Agile Combat Employment [ACE] concept of operations and now incorporate off-station training on the student's third and fourth scheduled sortie as an 'out and back' trip. They land at nearby Randolph as a means of managing risk. If something breaks, we can at least get to Randolph, get the pilots back and get our maintainers over there to fix the jet. The

idea is to demystify landing somewhere other than Lackland so if they must divert to some place other than planned, it's not the first time they're doing it. That's probably the closest we've got to the ACE concept."

Weapons

Of the B-course, Cienski said: "We focus on the basic course. We teach them how to manoeuvre in relation to another airplanes, manoeuvre in relation to the ground and then drop munitions, employ the gun, shoot IR-guided and radar-guided missiles and then drop IR-guided and GPS-guided munitions. So, when you're teaching them how to drop a Small Diameter Bomb, the interface looks slightly different, but you've got to check to make sure the GPS is working, that you have the right steer point, and you have the right profile on the bomb. Those procedures

Above: **Two F-16s assigned to the 149th FW approach a KC-135R Stratotanker from the 155th Air Refueling Wing, Lincoln ANG Base, Nebraska, for aerial refuelling.** US Air National Guard/ Airman 1st Class Derek Gutierrez

Below: **An F-16 from the 149th FW prepares to receive fuel from a KC-135R Stratotanker from Nebraska ANG's 155th Air Refueling Wing.** US Air National Guard/Airman 1st Class Derek Gutierrez

all translate well to employing other weapons in their subsequent training. We're teaching them the basics, so when they get to their combat unit, they're going to learn how to get to the target, find the target and drop on the target, whether they took off from home station or an outfield. That's part of their continued learning.

"Students don't shoot any missiles, but we try to arrange for them to drop laser-guided and GPS-guided bombs, and dumb BDU-33s. At the local range we can strafe, employ BDU-33s, heavy 500lb dumb bombs and laser-guided bombs. The only munition type we can't drop at our local range are those with GPS guidance because of the greater release footprint required. The area of land of our range is not big enough to incorporate all the safety margins, so we drop GPS-guided weapons at Fort Hood – Fort Cavazos [Texas]."

State Partnership Programme

Discussing the ANG's state partnership programme, Lt Col Cienski said: "The Texas ANG has three state partners – Chile, the Czech Republic and Egypt. Seven years ago, we went to Chile, and eight years ago, went to the Czech Republic. We have also sent instructor pilots to Egypt to conduct aft cockpit air refuelling and night-vision goggles training. Instead of sending our jets to Egypt, we complete annual engagements by either sending pilots to Egypt or hosting pilots and other individuals from any of our state partners. In 2023, I went to the Czech Republic and flew with the Czech Air Force in the L-159, talked

about mission planning and reviewed basic tactics."

Addressing the 149th's training requirements, Cienski said: "This year we're hoping to align our own requirements and those of the CRTCs by finding a better solution for deploying to Savannah, Biloxi, Volk or Alpena by moving from air-to-ground to air-to-air training, because it costs a lot of money to move bombs to different CRTC locations.

"When we deployed to Alpena last August, two tankers dragged us up there, one of which remained for the week to enable daily aerial refuelling training. We also incorporated the tanker as a simulated bomber for the DCA fight. Alpena [Michigan] offers a lot of air space and over water training. That required us to refresh our water survival training and fly with a life preserver and locator, which we don't use when flying from Lackland."

B-course specifics

Mention of the B-course throughout this feature refers to Air Education and Training Command's F-16 basic course run by Lt Col Cienski and his colleagues.

The course comprises five phases:

- Transition
- Basic fighter manoeuvring (BFM)
- Tactical intercepts
- Basic surface attack
- Precision-guided weapon employment

Culmination of the B-course is a large force exercise in which the students fight their way to their target, drop precision-guided bombs from medium altitude and then fight their way out.

Above: **A 149th FW crew chief marshals an F-16 at Davis-Monthan Air Force Base, Arizona.** US Air National Guard/ Airman 1st Class Derek Gutierrez

Transition and BFM

Students start their course with six weeks of academics before flying training begins, it's a scripted phase just like any other pipeline training.

Simulators are interspersed throughout flying training to introduce each new event and role. The initial academics often seem overwhelming to the student

Right: **An F-16 assigned to the Texas ANG's 149th FW flies alongside a KC-135 Stratotanker from Air Force Reserve Command's 507th Refueling Wing based at Tinker Air Force Base, Oklahoma.** US Air National Guard/Airman 1st Class Derek Gutierrez

because of the number of workbooks, classes and simulators before the student can set foot in a jet. Throughout the course, students rely on civilian and military instructors who are well placed make sense of the course from the early stage.

In the first part, the student was introduced to the techniques required to take off, land, fly and cruise. Instructor pilots (IPs) follow the student around the pattern and tell them to go around if something unsafe is observed. Once a student pilot completes their check ride, they receive their initial Form 8, a certificate that shows they can safely pilot the aircraft in daytime visual and instrument conditions.

Students are then introduced to tactics starting with basic fighter manoeuvring: low aspect, followed by high aspect and then nose-to-nose BFM. These require a wider array of personal techniques, imparted to the students by different IPs.

Generally, pilots rate the F-16 as an aircraft that is not too hard to learn to fly, but hard to learn to fight, especially

Liz Kaszynski / Lockheed Martin

Above: **A P-47 Thunderbolt and an F-16 overfly San Antonio as part of the 182nd FS's 60th anniversary celebration: the fighter squadron flew P-47s in combat during World War Two.** US Air Force/SMSgt Mike Arellano

Below: **The 149th FW's 182nd Fighter Squadron (FS) hosted a large force exercise with the 457th FS from Fort Worth at JBSA–Lackland on May 21, 2022. The event involved modernised tactics of fourth and fifth-generation aircraft in advanced aerial combat.** US Air National Guard/SSgt Ryan Mancuso

when they try to use the controls on the throttle and stick to command the jet to do what they want: that's a challenge.

The air force uses a basic left hand–right hand instruction technique. An IP takes the student through the mission brief and instructs them at the start of the aerial battle to select max afterburner with their left hand, and with their right hand to roll out and fly to where the adversary starts their turn. When the student reaches that point, they must start their turn by pulling to 9G with their right hand and relax to freeze the adversary so they can start to decrease angles that will allow them to attack from a stable gunshot position.

That sequence happens in about five to seven seconds, so the student's hands and brain will not function as fast as required. Because of the air combat manoeuvring instrumentation system used by the air force, the IP and the student can use the mission data recorded during the flight in the debrief. This enables the IP to identify when the student carried out the IP's instructions. For example, the student may have selected max afterburner

a little too late or pulled too hard when they needed to relax and apply back-stick pressure instead of pointing at the adversary.

During a BFM sortie, the tactical portion lasts for no more than 20 minutes but the debrief lasts about two hours. The 20-minute tactical portion in the first few BFM rides is a script. The student may be soaked in sweat, breathing hard and will be barely hanging on by the end. The IP must get him to take a deep breath and prepare to return to Lackland and land as they did in the transition phase. Students fly three offensive BFM flights. Generally, students struggle with the first two, but on the third, nearly all students perform better.

Air Combat Manoeuvring

The training programme is designed to cater for an average student such that if an individual gets to the end of the BFM phase, the IPs can safely move them on to air combat manoeuvring (ACM). This primarily comprises 2 v 1 and 2 v 2 engagements, which require them to deconflict with a third and a fourth aircraft.

In a similar way to the start of the BFM phase, IPs find that the student's hands and brain do not function quickly enough, so the IPs must figure out where the lags are and speed up the execution. IPs try to make things as simple as they can for the students, so they have the brain capacity to keep up with what's going on. By primarily calling 'left hand', 'right hand' on the radio, the IP can get things to a simple state.

An IP can adapt each flight based on the student's ongoing performance. Some perform well, such that the IP can fly more aggressively against them – as if flying against another instructor. For

A crew chief signals the pilot to apply the brakes at Hickam AFB, Hawaii, after an air-to-air mission during Exercise Sentry Aloha. US Air Force/TSgt Shane Cuomo

students who are struggling, the IP keeps it simple and gets them to the minimum standard required by the air force.

Tactical Intercepts

Following ACM, students move on to long-range tactical intercepts (TIs), which train them to use the aircraft's radar to identify, target and shoot missiles to kill the adversary. Up to this point in the course, the student has visually manoeuvred the aircraft in relation to another.

Students start with basic 1 v 1 long-range intercepts and then step up to 2 v 2 and finally 4 v 4. In the complicated 4 v 4 scenarios, IPs want the student to remain in formation and follow the flight lead as they execute the tactics. If the student can achieve that with a shot or two, it's good. If the student can do that and shoot multiple contacts at the same time, they are doing well.

The TI phase culminates with a defensive counter-air (DCA) mission in which the student is responsible for protecting a target. During the mission, adversaries may fly at low-level to test the student to look down low as per the radar tactics instruction given to them.

Before the DCA mission, IPs spend a significant amount of time teaching academics and having informal one-on-one conversations with the students to ensure they understand what's going to happen, their

Above: **An F-16 fighter pilot assigned to the 149th FW taxis to the runway at Lackland, Texas.** US Air National Guard/SSgt Derek Gutierrez

responsibilities, the importance of the sortie and the instructor's expectations.

In the air-to-air portion, which represents about half the training programme, the aircraft is configured in one of two ways. One configuration is referred to as a centreline bag jet fitted with just one fuel tank on the centreline station. This configuration is used mostly for air-to-air training. The configuration changes for the final portion of air-to-air training when the sorties are longer, which requires a bigger fuel payload provided by two external fuel tanks

carried under-wing; a configuration referred to as a two-bag jet.

Air-to-Ground

Before transitioning to the air-to-ground phase, students complete low-level step-down training to learn how to fly at 500ft and safely manoeuvre near the ground. Aircraft are configured as two-bag jets throughout the air-to-ground phase.

This phase requires the carriage of both laser and GPS-guided bombs, which causes a lot of information to be

presented to the student. Much of that information is not relevant to the training requirements of the flight, so the IPs try to cage the student's thinking into understanding what they must do to make the bomb hit the target.

IPs have extensive discussions with the student about a valid versus an invalid weapon employment. When dropping a GPS-guided weapon on a set of co-ordinates, it's vital for the student to realise they can induce a slew into the guidance system by accidentally bumping a switch. Should that happen, the guidance system thinks the target is not at the point given by the co-ordinates.

Students must follow in-depth Traffic, Alert and Collision Avoidance System (TCAS) laser checks: T reminds them to switch the tapes on; C reminds them to place their cursor to zero to remove any slew out of the system; A reminds them to check the jet's altitude mode. The checks ensure that the pilot has the right laser code. Different aircraft in a flight have different laser codes. Therefore, if the pilot laser-designates for one jet and then his own, but without resetting the laser coding for his jet, then the bomb will never detect the laser energy.

If a bomb malfunctions in combat and doesn't go where it's supposed to, the tapes will be checked to make sure the pilot applied the TCAS checks properly. If the pilot doesn't complete a proper check, they could miss the intended or

Right: **A pilot lifts his flight helmet prior to launch during Coronet Cactus at Davis-Monthan Air Force Base, Arizona, in April 2023. The annual training event deploys members of the 149th FW to another base to familiarise them with accomplishing mission objectives in an unfamiliar location.** US Air National Guard/ TSgt Derek Davis

Left: **F-16C 87-255/SA painted with a tail marking once displayed on the 149th FW's aircraft.** US Air Force

kill innocent people. IPs must ensure each student completes the course with a full understanding that when they hit the pickle button, they are striking the right target.

Close air support (CAS), a primary role for the F-16, is introduced towards the end of the air-to-ground portion. Typically, CAS missions are aligned with the final large force employment exercise. The student flies a strike mission as part of an eight-ship that must fight adversaries on the way into the target area, find the proper target, conduct the TCAS check, drop the valid weapon and then fight adversaries on the way out. This is the capstone exercise of the B-course and for a trainee multi-role fighter pilot.

Explaining why the syllabus changes, Cienski said: "We take feedback from the combat air forces and work through rewrites of the syllabus every couple of years. Tactics change based on the perceived threats; we must train for

a great power competition against near-peer adversaries. We must be prepared for the changing nature of the conflicts that the US and its allies might end up in, so we change what we're training people to do, but overall, the initial qualification course [the B-course] tends to stay roughly the same. We teach a new pilot how to fly the jet, how to do dog-fighting, how to do 2 v 1, how to do tactical intercepts, elements that stay the same… it's the numbers that change as the potential threats change."

The most significant addition in recent years was precision-guided weapon delivery, the provision of more rounds for practising strafing and the close air support component.

The 149th's first B-course class began in May 2000 and to this day, as a formal training unit, it continues to qualify skilled and qualified F-16 fighter pilots to bases around the world.

PEGGY IN NEW ENGLAND

Fully equipped with the KC-46 Pegasus tanker aircraft, New Hampshire Air National Guard's 157th Air Refueling Wing is busy supporting Air Mobility Command and US Transport Command daily

STAFF SERGEANT AARON Flynn is a KC-46 crew chief serving with the 157th Maintenance Group (MXG). His day-to-day work involves scheduled-, flying-, and A-check inspections. He also conducts pre-launch checks to ensure the aircraft is ready for flight with the correct levels of oil and hydraulic fluid, the tyres are good, and it is loaded with the required amount of fuel.

As a crew chief, Flynn is also involved with aircraft preparation for temporary duty (TDY) away from Pease, washing an aircraft or performing A-check maintenance. The latter involves general visual inspections, lubricating components, some functional tests, and built-in tests.

Ease of Maintenance

Flynn previously served with Maine Air National Guard's 101st Maintenance Group working on the iconic KC-135R Stratotanker. Based on his tanker experience, Flynn described the KC-46 as: "An absolute dream to work on by comparison to the KC-135. Anytime there's an issue with an electrical system or there's a mechanical problem somewhere on the jet, a code is sent to the flight deck through the central maintenance computing function [CMCF] which displays the code. We use a fault isolation manual that takes me through, step-by-step, whether to replace the component, the need to run a bit test or not, and providing different avenues for troubleshooting. Crew chiefs troubleshoot to the extent we can, then we delegate it off to whoever's the expert in that field. The fault code index is one of the best tools we have on the KC-46.

According to Flynn, most such components are easy to change and within reach of the ground, using JLG high lifts for very specific tasks.

He said: "Having worked on the KC-135, including a couple of deployments, and I can't recall the number times I've spent hours if not days on end, trying to troubleshoot mechanical issues trying to figure out what's wrong with the aircraft. The KC-46 will, if it doesn't indicate exactly what's wrong, get you close enough to troubleshoot a few areas to narrow it down.

"Our aircraft maintenance manuals are good and comprehensive, but

Below: **Airmen from various aeromedical evacuation squadrons prepare a KC-46 Pegasus for aeromedical evacuation familiarization training at St Paul, Minnesota.** US Air National Guard/Amy Lovgren

Above: **Engine mechanics with the 157th Maintenance Group, suspend an auxiliary power unit with fishing pole lifting equipment at Pease Air National Guard Base.** US Air National Guard/ SSgt Victoria Nelson

they are written for the airframe and powerplant mechanic working for a commercial operator because this plane is an FAA [Federal Aviation Administration] commercial derivative aircraft.

"The KC-135 technical orders are very step-by-step; they tell you exactly what to do. By comparison, the KC-46 operates with the assumption that the maintainer already knows a lot about working the aircraft. For example, it might say remove the component, which assumes the mechanic knows or can determine how to remove the hardware without being told exactly what to do.

Landing Away and TDY

According to Flynn, if a KC-46 lands at an unexpected location, he can still turn the aircraft without any kind of support equipment. As a crew chief on the first KC-46 to participate in an exercise with KC-135s, he explained: "Not understanding how the KC-46 operates, transient alert brought a power cart out to the aircraft just as they do with KC-135s. We advised them we have an APU [auxiliary power unit] and, provided we have fuel, we'll be good to go.

"Our jets fly well. In my experience, they almost always land as code one [the term for no maintenance write-ups], and

Right: **Engine mechanics with the 157th Maintenance Group, lower an auxiliary power unit with fishing pole lifting equipment during the first full replacement of an APU on a KC-46.** US Air National Guard/ SSgt Victoria Nelson

typically, when they do return code two or code three, it's usually not a very big issue to fix."

When 157th ARW KC-46s deploy on TDY, the typical mix of maintenance personnel comprises a lead crew chief, a secondary crew chief, and an avionics airman to maintain its computer systems. Augmenting that mix on longer TDYs, are airmen from the electrical and environmental shops, and hydraulics for fighter drags.

Flynn said: "Each time we use the centreline drogue system, we need to reel it out, inspect it, and reel it back in. We usually take an airman from hydraulics to assist because they are the experts."

Surprisingly, the KC-46 does not deploy with any kind of maintenance pack or spare tyres, but typically oil and hydraulic fluid, and a spare bulb rack. An extra set of landing and wing root lights are taken on longer routes.

When operating from hot and very cold locations, the aircraft's integrated heating and cooling system, which is part of the onboard inert gas generating system, serves as an air conditioner and heater. This enables the aircraft to heat or cool itself on the flight line of locations that endure searing heat or plummeting temperatures.

Flight Control

One notable achievement completed by the 157th Maintenance Group took place at Pease Air National Guard Base on October 5, 2023: repair and reclamation mechanics completed the first full replacement of a flight control surface on a KC-46.

Airmen replaced the left outboard elevator, a flight control surface on the tail that controls the angle of the nose (pitch) of the aircraft causing it to climb or dive during flight. The removal and installation took the team two full days and one week of preparation.

Commenting at the time, Master Sergeant Adam Hart, repair and reclamation lead with the 157th Maintenance Group said: "It requires rigging of flight controls that don't normally get replaced. We are also working through everything for the first time. It's new to everyone and we must be extra cognisant of the different parts and everyone's roles. A KC-46 elevator is about the size of an F-16 wing."

Cargo Capability

A KC-46 can carry a mixed cargo load comprising pallets placed either side-by-side or along the centreline, with the floor configured accordingly.

Compared to cargo aircraft such as the C-17, which are fitted with heavy rigid floors, the KC-46 was primarily designed to save fuel, so its floor is made of composite material. That precludes the KC-46 from carrying extremely heavy pieces of cargo but does allow carriage of 18 463L pallets and palletised passenger seat kits.

The entire floor can also be configured for the medevac mission, both overseas and on a regular basis in the United States, for patients who must be moved to a different medical facility.

Located on the left side of the forward fuselage, the cargo door is easy to operate, with just an unlock switch to open the 11ft wide door which hydraulically locks itself in place once it reaches its open position.

The cargo door features downward-pointing lights built-in for any kind of dusk or night-time operations. Extending from the door, the cargo hold is well-lit by bright LED lights.

A Checks

A military derivative of the commercial 767, the KC-46 follows a commercial-based A check maintenance schedule. Each KC-46 aircraft undergoes a different A check every two months. The frequency is based on the type's FAA certification and what's considered the lowest number of flying hours for an A check.

During the first year of its A check schedule, an aircraft undergoes a 1A, 2A, 3A, 4A, 5A and 6A checks. The exact checks get repeated for the second year, but these are labelled 7A, 8A, 9A, 10A, 11A, and 12 is a C check which is undertaken by the Oklahoma Air Logistics Center (OC-ALC) at Tinker Air Force Base.

During the author's visit to Pease, one KC-46 was undergoing its 9A check, equivalent to a 3A check, in the first year. For a crew chief, a 9A check requires lubricating the main and nose landing gear components, general visual inspections, and fuel checkout tests. The jet shop checks engine components, oil levels, and chip detectors.

This schedule is deemed to be stout for the number of flying hours each 157th Aircraft Refueling Wing (ARW) KC-46 undertakes in two months. To invoke change to the schedule, the 157th MXG brought experts from Atlanta-based Delta TechOps for advice on invoking change.

Flynn said the 157th MXG is evaluating the impacts of extending the period between checks. He said: "We're currently in the process of potentially increasing the regularity from every two months to every six months to better match our level of flying. That helps to save on manpower, man hours, consumables, and component usage."

The KC-46 does not undergo the more in-depth isochronal (ISO) inspections conducted every 24 months, 1,800 hours of flight or 1,100 landings. An ISO inspection takes multiple phases and multiple specialty codes to complete. That's because the nature of the aircraft is its FAA certification. To satisfy the

Above: **Fuerza Aerea Colombiana Kfir C2s fly in formation with a KC-46 during Exercise Relampago VII for joint interoperability training.** US Air National Guard/ MSgt Nicole Szews

Left: **A 157th Air Refueling Wing structural maintenance airman paints a 16ft-tall Minute Man on the tail of the Spirit of Portsmouth, a KC-46A assigned to the wing.** US Air National Guard/SMSgt Timm Huffman

Left: **A KC-46A Pegasus assigned to the 157th Air Refueling Wing performs an aerial demonstration at Pease Air National Guard Base.** US Air National Guard/TSgt Steven Tucker

FAA certification, the KC-46 undergoes various regular inspections, scheduled maintenance requirements and certification maintenance requirements.

System Maintenance

A boom check is completed every two weeks. The probe is extended while in the maintenance mode to check the pressure. Heavy boom maintenance is led by the hydraulics and fuel shops.

The 157th MXG undertook the first boom swap in the spring of 2021, with oversight provided by the quality assurance (QA) shop and Boeing field service representatives.

The 157th's hydraulic shop was heavily involved in the re-assembly of the boom, and its reinstallation.

In mid-October, engine mechanics with the 157th MXG completed the first full replacement of an auxiliary power unit (APU) on a KC-46. An APU is a small engine installed in the back of the KC-46 aircraft providing power to start the main engines. It also generates electrical and

compressed air power used to run the heating, cooling, and ventilation systems prior to starting the main engines. In the event of engine failure during flight, it can be used for either electrical power or bleed air to restart the engines.

The unserviceable APU was vibrating excessively and causing duct work to shake. The team replaced it with a similar model using fishing-pole lifting equipment and a small crane

Below: **A KC-46A assigned to the 157th Air Refueling Wing at Joint Base Elmendorf-Richardson, Alaska, in the wing's heritage paint scheme showcasing the wing's National Guard history in the state of New Hampshire.** US Air National Guard/SMSgt Timm Huffman

to extract the first engine, keeping it suspended while they transferred parts to the new unit.

This was the first time a brand-new APU was taken from supply and installed on a KC-46 by USAF personnel across the entire community.

Flight Deck

Thanks to KC-46 Air Refueling Operator (ARO) (boomer) Master Sergeant Nate Tarleton and KC-46 pilot Major Matt Rouleau, the author got to see the flight deck, ARO and cargo hold of a KC-46 assigned to the 157th ARW.

Interesting fact number one: outside of air refuelling procedures, the boom operator tends to occupy one of the flight deck jump seats which provides a third person to make radio calls and another set of eyes in the flight deck.

The captain sits on the left and the first officer on the right. The seat allocations are interchangeable because the controls are the same, meaning the aircraft can be flown from either seat.

The flight deck houses mission systems as well as a unique-to-the-KC-46 fuel panel which enables the pilot to control or jettison fuel. That said, the fuel system automatically adjusts the fuel by distributing it between tanks: on the KC-135, the pilot must track and adjust that manually.

Explaining, Rouleau said: "We key the amount of fuel we expect to upload into the computer, and it calculates where to distribute the fuel to adjust the centre of gravity [CG] to keep within limits – same thing when we're offloading. Maintaining the aircraft's CG is important for its stability and efficiency in flight."

Three autopilots are positioned on the console, one on the left, one in the centre, and one on the right. "Theoretically, we can take off manually and as soon as we hit 400ft turn an autopilot on. Provided

we've programmed everything correctly, while monitoring, we can allow it to climb, level off, fly the route, and land itself at the destination," said Rouleau.

Four identical and interchangeable screens dominate the flight deck. On each one, the pilot can pull up a synoptic display, showing for example, fuel. While fuel is uploading on the aircraft, the fuel display turns green and shows exactly which tanks the fuel is being carried in. While fuel is being offloaded, the fuel display shows the cumulative quantity, and each tank displays its own CG. The display also shows fuel being cross-fed from one engine to another.

Fact number two: despite the two powerful Pratt & Whitney 4062 engines each rated with 62,000lb of thrust, the KC-46 flight deck is much quieter than expected. And because of the bountiful amount of insulation installed around the flight deck and throughout the aircraft, aircrew can hear each other across the cockpit without the need for headset.

Aircrew serving with the 157th ARW said the KC-46 flight deck is more comfortable than a KC-135 because of the seats and four different temperature zones, each controlled to one degree of temperature.

According to Rouleau, pilots don't feel so tired at the end of a flight because the autopilot capability removes the need to continually fly the aircraft manually, instead they simply manage the systems.

During air refuelling, autopilot enables the pilot to set altitude and airspeed. If engaged when flying a racetrack pattern, the autopilot commands the constant turns while the pilot monitors. However, despite the benefits, autopilot cannot be engaged with certain aircraft types in certain situations.

Coronet Planning

Rouleau is a full-time Coronet planner working with a dedicated office at Pease, one of only four such offices in the USAF. "From a Coronet planner standpoint, the KC-46 is more advantageous than the KC-135 because of its take-off and landing performance. One, we can take-off with more fuel than a KC-135, that's at max gross weight every single time, whatever the location. With the KC-135, we are always concerned about getting off the ground with a maximum fuel load, which is always a game time decision on whether that would happen or not.

"Depending on the size of the cell, and the amount of offload the fighters need, we typically plan a KC-135 for the round robin. The aircraft departs either Pease or Bangor, completes the first two or three offloads, and then returns to Bangor. And [we] typically plan a KC-46 to do the bulk of the offload, dragging them over the ocean and perform the mission commander role for that cell. We frequently use SATCOM, which is like using a phone to call ahead to our destination airfield, get weather, pass along information, maintenance status, all well ahead of any radio range, so it's very beneficial. If necessary, we also plan for another tanker positioned at Prestwick to meet the fighters and drag them the rest of the way.

"Two, we can reduce the moderate turbulence gradient because of the aircraft's rating. So, the KC-46 can undertake air refuelling in moderate turbulence. However, if there's anything greater than trace icing, air refuelling cannot be conducted. Trace icing is a rate of ice accumulation slightly greater than the rate of ice loss due to sublimation.

"We typically have 3,000ft altitude in the altitude reservation [which allows use of airspace under prescribed conditions], so we can descend below or climb above the baseline altitude by 1,000ft to avoid icing. If that doesn't work, we can request a deviation to the left or the right, of course.

"Based on the better performance of the KC-46's weather radar compared to the KC-135, pilots are provided with the weather condition ahead of the aircraft's position which allows them to plan, which is a big advantage.

"As a tanker aircraft, the KC-46 is more stable for pilots flying the receiver aircraft. The 157th aircrew try to brief every receiver to be cognisant of the bow wave and the step room. That way, in the event there's a disconnect or breakaway, the pilots know when to pull their power to avoid an undershoot of the boom.

"On approach to land, the KC-46 is also stable and very responsive. When

Below: **KC-46A aircraft assigned to the 157th Air Refueling Wing perform an elephant walk formation on the runway at Pease Air National Guard Base on September 8, 2021.** US Air National Guard/SMSgt Timm Huffman

accounting for crosswind components that are affecting the aircraft, the pilot needs only to input pressure movements to the control stick. It crabs slightly when landing in a slight crosswind which is different to most aircraft that need to be aligned with the runway when touching down."

Air Refuelling Station

Talking through the layout of the air refuelling operator station, Tarleton explained that the left seat is the instructor position which has an override capability, and the right seat is the boom operator's position. The left screen repeats what's displayed on the right screen.

The remote vision system (RVS) screens are at the top of the console, the system comprises infrared panoramic cameras and three screens. Its capability includes display of each wingtip on the left and right screens. The depicted view can be changed to suit the conditions of the day, as can the camera's sensitivity.

Discussing the issues widely reported with the RVS, Tarleton stated: "Is it a perfect system? No. It can use some improvements. It has its limitations, but we're using it every day and can get the mission done.

"Conducting air refuelling using a video system meant a big change in culture. Both systems come with their pros and cons. Looking out the window is great but night-time air refuelling in a KC-135 can be difficult with tail-mounted floodlights and the need to dim everything on the boomer's control panel to prevent reflections in the screen. By comparison, night-time refuelling in the KC-46 is completely unmatched. The clear picture fed from the infrared camera system at night is unbelievable."

Positioned below the three screens is a main screen which displays a 3D view when selected and a centre panel which

has the camera selectors used to choose the camera and operate its focussing.

Tarleton explained: "Once a refuelling starts, we switch to our 3D camera. A door opens and two cameras [part of a different system] focus on a single point where the boom is lowered and extended. This gives depth perception when 3D glasses are used to get a clear picture. The scene and the setting from the 3D camera can be changed. Changes are required when the aircraft turns, and the position of the sun also changes.

"That's part of the RVS issue that everyone loves to talk about. Sometimes when using the 3D camera, we must send the receiver back and change the camera setting before we allow them to come back in."

Another panel is used to control the computer system itself for example, calling-up details about the boom or selecting the type of aircraft to be refuelled because each type has its limitations on where the boom flies. It automatically calls up the limitations of the aircraft type selected and changes the automatic disconnect capability for when an aircraft reaches those limitations. Tarleton said: "On the KC-135, we had to monitor analogue gauges and when close to a limitation, manually disconnect. On the KC-46 it's automated and projected on the screen, a green, orange, or red icon advises the status; green is good, orange is approaching danger, and red indicates to try again. When we select the aircraft type, it includes a pre-set lighting configuration to illuminate that type of aircraft correctly.

"If the aircraft develops any type of malfunction, the air refuelling system page provides guidance on where to start a diagnosis. Anytime there's

something that isn't normal, a message pops up telling the crew what to do. We run through a checklist. If it works, you're good. If it doesn't, we return to what the checklist tells you to do."

A sidestick controller is fitted on both sides of the console. The right sidestick flies the boom with up and down control to provide general azimuth and elevation. The left sidestick controls the probe telescoping, in and out. Once the boom is aligned with the receiver aircraft's receptacle, the probe is telescoped out to make contact. If contact fails, using the panel the boomer can command the system to make contact again. The controls are straightforward mostly comprising of switches to execute functions such as disconnect and pump manipulation. A panel housing the manual controls is also centrally positioned.

Once the aircraft type is entered into the system, the boom limitations for that type are set. When the probe contacts, the receiver aircraft's receptacle pumps energise automatically, as does shut down. While the probe is in contact with the receiver aircraft's receptacle, the system constantly aligns the boom with the receiver aircraft, so the boomer no longer needs to shadow the receiver as they fly around. The system corrects where it needs to be and keeps the boom aligned, which reduces fatigue for the boomer.

Commander's View

New Hampshire Air National Guard's 157th ARW is the first and only air guard KC-46 unit. Equipped with 12 aircraft, it's the only base, active-duty Air National Guard or Air Force Reserve, which has its full complement of KC-46s at this point.

Pease was announced in 2014 as the preferred location for the ANG's first KC-46 base. In January 2024, the USAF announced that Selfridge Air National Guard Base had been chosen

Below: **An elephant walk formation on the runway at Pease Air National Guard Base, the first such muster since receiving the KC-46.** US Air National Guard/ SMSgt Timm Huffman

as the second Air National Guard KC-46 base, while details of the third are still in abeyance.

In the subsequent years, Pease has undergone major construction to prepare the base for the KC-46, the first of which arrived at the massive New Hampshire base in August 2019.

The wing had to retool and refurbish many buildings on the base to accept new equipment. Two hangars underwent major modifications to house the height of the KC-46 tail. Configuration of the upgraded hangars is very different to the former KC-135 design. KC-46 support equipment is as much as four times the size of the equipment used for a KC-135. Part of the initial KC-46 build-up of Pease, the 157th ARW went through the process of divesting all the legacy equipment and receiving new equipment, a process led by the 157th Mission Support Group.

Chief Master Sergeant Erica Rhea, 157th ARW command chief, noted that the last KC-135 left Pease in March 2019 which required retention of equipment, supplies and parts until the aircraft left. "That required a huge effort by our equipment custodians the traffic management office and logistics," she said.

Explaining some of the construction, Colonel Nelson Perron, 157th ARW commander, said: "We had built a new squadron operations building while we were operating the KC-135R, but with the transition to the KC-46 and the added manning associated with hosting the active-duty 64th Air Refuelling Squadron, which joined in 2009 as a total force integration unit, that building is undergoing more renovations."

Not only a larger aircraft than the KC-135, but also a different type of aircraft, the KC-46 is modern, and its mission planning is based on a new

Above left: **A KC-135 boom is extended while a 157th ARW KC-46 closes on the probe during air refuelling training over the Atlantic.** US Air Force/Peter Borys

Above right: **A KC-46A Pegasus boom extended for an acceptance inspection.** US Air Force/A1C Alan Ricker

Right: **An aircraft maintainer with the 157th Maintenance Group, co-ordinates the removal of the flight control surface with the maintenance team and equipment operators at Pease Air National Guard Base, New Hampshire. This is the first time a brand-new flight control surface was taken from supply and installed by USAF personnel.** US Air National Guard/TSgt Victoria Nelson

way of thinking. The 157th Operations Group has a mission planning cell (MPC) which conducts all mission planning, a process that is more intensive for aircrew, hence the new facilities and equipment required for the KC-46.

Aircrew Training

The 157th Operations Group, which commands the 133rd Air Refueling Squadron, adopted a variety of different methods to train aircrew. Perron said: "We had one crew that was part of the initial operational test and evaluation force at Edwards Air Force Base to test different systems and procedures on how this aircraft would operate. They went to Miami, got a type rating on the 767, and then went to Boeing in Seattle to complete follow-on training.

"Most of our aircrew went to Altus Air Force Base, Oklahoma, and McConnell Air Force Base, Kansas for initial training. That was a three-month training window shared between a few weeks of academics, 18 simulators, a simulator check-ride, then four to seven mission-driven flights.

"The big difference with the KC-46 compared to the KC-135, is its capability to be air refuelled, a skill not many of our pilots had prior to transition, which presented them a big learning curve. As we grew our squadrons, we realised we needed to reach out to other communities with those skill sets to help in the transition."

Rhea said: "For our maintainers, some of whom had been operating the KC-135 for 30 years, transition to the KC-46 was a reset. About 30 maintainers assigned to the McConnell-based Mobile Training Team (MTT) came to Pease to teach 157th MXG personnel. It was more cost effective. The MTT started with the fundamental parts of the new tech orders and fundamentals of the aircraft, the basic avionics and hydraulic systems, because there was no aircraft at Pease at that time. Concurrently, our instructors were learning about the KC-46, which created a team effort of figuring things out within the online tech orders. When it comes to understanding all the systems, the components and how they work, this aircraft is a beast.

"After that, about 30 of our folks went to Altus Air Force Base for two to three months to get hands-on training, which was the first time they got to dig into the KC-46 aircraft. Upon their return, we relied on them to teach our folks returning from other bases."

Total Force Integration

The active-duty 64th Air Refueling Squadron (ARS) was assigned to Pease in 2009 where it operated as a total force integration (TFI) unit until the 157th ARW started its KC-46 transition. While the squadron flag remained at Pease, its people went to different Air Mobility Command bases to continue support to US TRANSCOM until the 157th was fully stood up with the KC-46. The 64th ARS was officially stood up at Pease on July 8, 2022, and as of late October, 42 of the eventual 159 airmen that will be a part of the squadron had returned. Some maintainers and aircrew are current and qualified in the KC-46.

Rhea said: "Some are returning from different weapon systems and require KC-46 training which they'll receive either at a main operating base or from MTT training here at Pease."

Reactivation of the active-duty 64th ARS is the first time the ANG has fielded a major weapon system concurrently with active-duty counterparts. "That's a big deal," stated Perron.

Remote Vision System

Asked about the widely reported issue with the KC-46, the remote vision system (RVS) and how it might be impacting operations, Perron said: "When we transitioned, many of our boom operators were concerned about the different way of doing business

Above: A KC-46A Pegasus, dubbed the Spirit of Portsmouth on July 1, 2022, emblazoned with a colourful paint scheme. US Air National Guard/SSgt Victoria Nelson

compared to a KC-135, which has a sighting door and a window between them and the receiver aircraft. Now we're using a camera system [RVS], a new evolution in technology that we must trust with 100% confidence.

"The current RVS system is very capable and we're able to conduct pretty much every mission set that we're tasked to do. In certain conditions, the KC-46 system is better than the KC-135 system.

"Air Mobility Command devised the employment concept exercise (ECE) which is a way to assess the confidence measures of the aircraft. This allowed us to put the aircraft into the system and in different areas test the supply chain, test the infrastructure in route support; things we needed to understand to bolster those confidence measures for the aircraft.

"Then we flew a mission, for example a complex move, like a Coronet* dragging receivers over the Atlantic. After we completed each mission, we followed-up with an after-action report, which was submitted to AMC [Air Mobility Command]

staff who studied the data to help them decide about releasing different subsets of missions. It has really accelerated what the KC-46 can do to this day. I have complete confidence in the system which will only get better with the enhanced RVS 2.0."

*A Coronet is a mission where aircraft that need to travel large distances, either over land or oceans, are assigned tankers to fly with them to provide fuel along their route.

Class of Tanker

Prior to its service entry, the USAF had two types of tankers to call upon: the tactical class KC-135 and the strategic class KC-10. Each class is based upon the type's fuel offload capacity. The KC-46 sits between the two, so the author asked Perron if the USAF will be short of strategic tankers when all the KC-10s have been withdrawn from service? He replied: "The fact that it can receive fuel in flight means we can force project or be force extended. If the KC-46 is tasked with a strategic type of mission that the KC-10 currently holds, we

Right: The unique flight on March 17, 2022, was women-only, from the two pilots to the maintainers, crew to air traffic control. US Air National Guard/SSgt Victoria Nelson

can do that if we have another tanker to top our tanks up in the appropriate time. This aircraft offers US TRANSCOM [United States Transportation Command] different capabilities, air refuelling, aeromedical evacuation, and airlift, so it's a very capable aircraft.

"We don't have to swap out the drogue system in between missions, litter stanchion systems are embedded in the aeroplane, and palletised airline-type seating can easily be rolled-on and rolled-off."

Pease: A Strategic Location

Pease is a strategic location to the great circle route going over the Atlantic. At two miles long, the runway is one of the largest in the northeast which facilitates a lot of operations.

Perron said: "On October 1, 2021, we stood up a team funded by the active-duty with 20-plus airmen assigned from operations, maintenance, logistics, and POL [petroleum, oils, and lubricants], who can be tasked by the 618th Air Operations Center based at Scott Air Force Base, Illinois, to support missions the KC-46 has been authorised to do.

He added: "Coronets depart from Pease and last year we flew over 750 hours in support of Coronet missions. We've had airmen deployed in Europe and the Pacific supporting exercises or operations to support the MAJCOMs [Major Commands] and AMC commanders.

"We conducted an ECE mission to Moron Air Base, Spain, in the spring. We flew training missions and some aerovac missions from Ramstein. Patients were flown back to the United States and,

as a confidence measure, we were able to conduct the mission from both an aircraft and flying point of view, and then submitted an after-action report, which led to us being able to fly those missions if tasked. We don't have an aeromedical evacuation squadron within the wing here at Pease. It's a mission that we're advocating for, but some people are trained and qualified to be assigned to Critical Care Air Transport Teams who fly on aerovac missions."

According to Perron, 157th ARW is unique for an air guard wing in a small state like New Hampshire because the KC-46 aircraft is not tasked a lot in support of the state. "We've already used the aircraft for the federal mission. We were called up for the Capitol response missions immediately after January 6 [2021], when we transported guardsmen in and out of the Capitol region."

Azorean Deployment

Between May 1 and 7, 2023, 250 airmen from the 157th ARW and the 64th Air Refueling Squadron (ARS) executed a large-scale, multi-day deployment to Lajes Air Base in the Azores, Portugal. The exercise was designed to test the wing's ability to provide rapid generation, employment, and sustainment of combat air power missions.

The unit maintained and operated four KC-46 aircraft, launched 19 sorties across the European theatre, simulated aeromedical evacuation operations, and tested the abilities of airmen to operate in new and uncertain circumstances, including simulated chemical warfare environments.

The training operation was led by New Hampshire Air National Guard but also involved aeromedical evacuation teams from Delaware, North Carolina, and Minnesota ANGs, a C-17 from the New York ANG, and a KC-135 from the Utah ANG.

The exercise started on May 1, as airmen arrived at Pease to complete just-in-time training and ensure they met all readiness requirements. Over the next three days, crews from across the base finalised documentation, assembled pallets, and configured and loaded cargo into the multiple KC-46 aircraft that launched. The training operation reached full-speed in the early hours of May 4, with airmen arriving as early as 0100hrs to out process prior to the four-hour flight to Lajes Air Base.

Within seven hours of the first take-off, the 157th ARW had launched eight of its KC-46 aircraft in support of the exercise and other operational taskings.

The drill was the 157th ARW's first deployment under the new Air Force Generation (AFFORGEN) model and tested the abilities of airmen to adapt to an unfamiliar location and uncertain situations. It also operationalized the agile combat environment (ACE) construct.

Training plans for the exercise were developed at the squadron level to allow leaders to tailor the exercise to the needs of their airmen. It also created unscripted circumstances that required decision making at the lowest level, using the information available, to meet exercise objectives – a key tenant of the ACE framework.

Below: **Every support role and operational role for flight PACK 81 was filled by women of the 157th Air Refueling Wing, on March 17, 2022.** US Air National Guard/SSgt Victoria Nelson

GUARDIANS
OF THE LAST
FRONTIER

Alaska Air National Guard's 168th Wing operates a fleet of KC-135R tanker aircraft on worldwide missions from Eielson Air Force Base, located on the top of the world

THE MEN AND women assigned to the 168th operate its KC-135R Stratotankers throughout the year in support of state, federal and overseas operations. Tasking includes an alert mission held at Eielson, 24/7, 365 days of the year, with a KC-135R aircraft and a crew ready to go at a moment's notice in support of North American Aerospace Defense Command. When launched, the alert tanker provides aerial refuelling to USAF F-22 Raptors and E-3 AWACS scrambled from Elmendorf Air Force Base at Anchorage and F-35A Lightning IIs from Eielson to intercept and monitor unknown aircraft approaching US airspace. Usually, the aircraft involved are Russian long-range bombers flying in international airspace, but near to the United States and Canada's Air Defense Interception Zone.

Russia has several arctic bases, the main one in the Russian far east is Ukrainka in Amur Oblast from where long-range bombers fly against Canadian and US

airspace, on what Russian authorities called combat patrols.

Alaska and Russia are separated by just 50 miles across the Bering Strait, which is where Russian bombers often fly and then run along either the Alaskan or Canadian northwest polar coastlines, or the Alaskan Pacific coastline.

Going On 65

The KC-135Rs assigned to Alaska Air Guard's tanker unit were built between 1959 and 1963. None of the guardsmen that hosted the author at the squadron's billets was born when their magnificent jets were built. However, the age of the aircraft is not given away by their state of repair and appearance. Sixty years old they may be, but these Alaskan 'birds' are all in tremendous condition thanks to the dedication of the maintainers and other guardsmen who work in all the back shops, often seven days a week, to generate aircraft ready to fly and support the wing's various missions.

The 168th Wing has over 800 authorised personnel of whom 350 are full-time; the balance comprises traditional guardsmen. Most of them live in Fairbanks, the main city close to Eielson, and Anchorage 350 miles to the south. The wing is a tenant unit at Eielson that undertakes federally funded operations in Title 10 of the US Code.

Daily training lines are undertaken when working for the state governor, most of them support the active-duty air force and its training missions, which helps with the 168th's training

War tasking is primarily conducted to support an air bridge to the Pacific theatre from Alaska, a very strategic region. Eielson is located at roughly an equal distance to Norfolk, Virginia, as it is to Tokyo, Japan. KC-135 aircrews can reach any destination in the northern hemisphere in roughly 12 hours from base flying to 75° North, on the great circle polar route.

Eielson serves as the primary staging airfield between the lower 48 and Asia, with the 168th handling aircraft going to or from Japan and the Korean peninsula.

The 168th is the only tanker unit based in Alaska, and is primarily a part-time force, yet it can fulfil between 40 and 50% of the requirements for aerial refuelling in Alaska and the northern Pacific. The balance of requirements is met by other units deploying to Eielson on temporary duty (TDY), which means the Alaskan guardsmen can train co-operatively with the visiting units.

Primary customers of the 168th are its sister air guard unit, the 176th Wing, and the two active-duty wings based in Alaska; the 3rd Wing at Elmendorf, and the 354th Fighter Wing, co-located at Eielson. The two active-duty wings have the greatest preponderance of aircraft so many of the 168th's aerial refuelling missions support both active-duty wings. Support is also provided to the various exercises held in Alaska, Red Flag, Northern Edge, and Distant Frontier.

Another facility manned by 168th personnel is a radar site located 60 miles to the west of Eielson that conducts space surveillance, detecting information after a missile launch, and cataloguing satellites and space junk.

Below: **KC-135R Stratotanker 63-8876 assigned to the 168th Wing, Alaska Air National Guard, taxies along the Eielson Air Force Base runway for an aerial refuelling mission during Exercise Red Flag-Alaska 24-3.** US Air National Guard/ SMSgt Julie Avey

Sub-Zero Maintenance

Aircraft maintenance during the winter at Eielson is brutal as the ambient air temperature can dip as low as -50°C. Driving snow is a regular weather condition.

Maintainers assigned to the 168th Aircraft Maintenance Squadron who work on aircraft parked on the flightline take rest cycles in the wing's building to warm up and make use trucks that run all day to keep them warm. Specialised clothing is essential and includes thick coveralls, bibs, jackets, gloves, hats, and winter boots.

The use of metal tools is closely managed. Crew chiefs keep the tools on board the warmed-up aircraft, while specialists from any of the squadron's back shops who come out to an aircraft bring their tools with them.

Aircraft require preheating for three hours before engine start to prevent failures capable of preventing the jet from taking off. Consequently, the aircraft maintenance squadron operates a mid-shift whose personnel preheat the aeroplane on the flight line. This involves placing 16 heaters on the undercarriage struts, the crew ladder, and the nose to keep the electronics warm, and the aft hatch to keep the cargo area warm. As a result of this procedure, personnel working the subsequent day shift arrive to launch a warmed-up aircraft.

The heaters used are aerospace ground equipment (AGE) heaters fitted with 12in diameter hoses that supply the warm air to the required position on the aircraft.

Above: An Alaska Air National Guard KC-135R Stratotanker conducts aerial refuelling with an F-16C Fighting Falcon during Exercise Red Flag Alaska 24-3. US Air National Guard/ SMSgt Julie Avey

If heat were not placed on the aircraft a couple of hours before take-off, when the flight crew stepped on the crew ladder the boom windows will crack because of the stiffness of the fuselage. Because the aircraft flies at altitude in sub-zero temperatures, the aircraft itself can handle the cold. The challenge is keeping people and support equipment warm, and initially getting the aircraft thawed.

If the crew were to taxi the aircraft out without heat having been applied on the struts, seals within the struts would blow, causing a three-day maintenance effort costing $12,000.

The lower nose bay houses avionics and electronics which are also heated for two hours before engine start to prevent computers from crashing or circuit breakers popping.

Fuel, Fluids and Engine Oil

Sub-zero conditions affect aviation fuel, such that the maintainers become concerned when the temperature drops to -45°C, which is close to the gel freeze point of the fuel. At Eielson, negative temperatures occur throughout the winter but tend to be lowest in January and February when it can drop to as low as -50°C for up to two weeks.

Servicing the aircraft before and after a flight in such temperatures also presents physical challenges. Standard engine oil used on the KC-135R will solidify to varying states from semi-fluid to a sticky and thick viscosity, depending on the ambient temperature, so the 168th runs with a different grade of engine oil [to other KC-135 units] that retains the required viscosity.

Cold is not the only adverse condition at Eielson; maintenance crews also have the additional burden of operating in extended darkness throughout the winter months. Every maintainer uses headlamps and flashlights, and if required mobile lights are used to illuminate the aircraft.

Maintenance Types

Most of the KC-135Rs assigned to the 168th have between 20,000 and 25,000 hours on their clocks, which are typical figures in the KC-135 fleet. The bigger

KC-135R Stratotanker 60-0334 in sub-zero conditions with heaters attached to warm the aircraft up before the aircrew arrives. US Air National Guard/SMSgt Julie Avey

takes between six and eight weeks to complete. It involves stripping the aircraft down to allow inspection of numerous essential systems. Inspection crews continually discover faults and conditions not seen before.

The 168th Maintenance Group has adopted predictive maintenance procedures using a system called CDM Plus, issued by the Oklahoma City depot (OC-AC). The process, originally used by Delta Airlines, involves using historical data of specific components to try and predict when each will fail and to change a component before it does fail: an effort to increase the aircraft's availability and mission capable rate.

Most unscheduled maintenance requirements on the KC-135R involve hydraulic and fuel leaks, and avionics systems, particularly communication control modules. The scheduling office tracks the maintenance requirements for each aircraft, which include things as diverse as battery changes and the lap belts used by the flight crew.

According to a senior maintainer assigned to the 168th Maintenance Group: "The KC-135, as old as it is, given the climate we endure during the winter, holds up really well."

problem is the chronological age of the jet, corrosion being the biggest associated issue, particularly on the keel beam and in the wheel wells.

The KC-135 depot at Oklahoma City Air Logistics Center, is encountering more structural issues on aircraft entering their six-year programmed depot maintenance (PDM). Consequently, engineering teams from the depot visit a unit to inspect an aircraft during a standard isochronal (ISO) inspection to get an early look at the aircraft to determine if anything significant is evident before it goes into the PDM cycle.

ISO inspections are conducted by the operating unit every 24 months and are a major maintenance event that

Above: **An airman de-ices a KC-135R at Eielson Air Force Base.** US Air National Guard/ SMSgt Julie Avey

A KC-135R Stratotanker at Eielson Air Force Base is prepared for an aerial refueling mission by airmen assigned to the 168th Aircraft Maintenance Squadron. US Air National Guard/SMSgt Julie Avey

JERSEY

Atlantic City Air National Guard Base is the home station of New Jersey Air National Guard's 177th Fighter Wing equipped with F-16C Fighting Falcons

Below: **F-16C 86-309/AC assigned to the 119th Fighter Squadron bearing the Jersey Jerk flagship tail flash at Atlantic Air National Guard. The aircraft is dedicated to USAF Major General Donald Strait, a former commander of the New Jersey Air National Guard, who flew a P-47 Thunderbolt, and a P-51 Mustang of the same name.** US Air National Guard/SrA Darion Boyd

DEVILS

LOCATED LESS THAN 150 miles south of New York City, Atlantic City International Airport in New Jersey is a busy commercial airport. The site also hosts the Atlantic City Air National Guard Base, home to the 177th Fighter Wing (FW) part of New Jersey Air National Guard. Equipped with Block 30 F-16C Fighting Falcons operated by the 119th Fighter Squadron, the unit traces its history to June 1917 and the 5th Aviation School Squadron. In October 1962, the 177th Tactical Fighter Group was activated, with the 119th Tactical Fighter Squadron as its flying component. Subsequent redesignations were the 177th Fighter Interceptor Group in January 1973, 177th Fighter Group in March 1992, and 177th FW in October 1995.

Lieutenant Colonel Michael Miles Long is the current commander of the 177th Operations Group (OG) and a seasoned F-16 pilot. Explaining the wing, Long said: "We train for two main missions. One, overseas contingency operations, training for near peer conflict in offensive counter air, close air support, surface attack, and defensive counter air Two, homeland defence for which we stand on alert here at our home station for the homeland defence mission, ready to go on a moment's notice. Our alert is tasked to defend down to South Carolina and up to New England. Our daily training revolves around the two mission sets, and each time we fly, we pick a specific mission and specific objectives, to maximize training in missions tailored to those two mindsets."

With concurrent alert tasking and general operations, 177th FW commanders must be cognisant of optimizing the right people and the equipment to complete all its training objectives complete.

Explaining the awareness required, Colonel Brian Cooper the 177th Maintenance Group commander said: "From the maintenance group's perspective, that balance is felt every day. Prepping jets to go to the alert facility requires a more rigorous aircraft generation process. If an issue pops up on an alert aircraft, everything stops on

A crew chief with the 177th Fighter Wing, prepares an F-16C at Boca Chica Field, Florida, during a training deployment. US Air National Guard/SMSgt Andrew Moseley

now consistently generate a six-turn-four schedule, which is impressive when compared to where we once were. Every week our pilots, maintainers, logistics, supply chain personnel, meet for an hour to discuss aircraft availability and pilot currencies in detail to ensure we're all operating from the same page. That gives us a full understanding of where we are as a wing, not just as ops or maintenance or supply, but collectively together to make sure we can meet the next week's objectives."

All the wings assigned F-16s are over 35 years old which makes it harder for the 177th Maintenance Group to get parts. That is not unique to the F-16 because every aircraft type has challenges with parts supply. The solution depends on the daily flying schedule to produce a replacement aircraft for the alert. We're constantly doing that around the clock, every day of the year to keep aircraft on alert status. Outside of such an incident, we must keep enough aircraft available on the flight line to meet the needs of the flight schedule every day, which generally comprises two turns.

"When I first joined this wing, on some days we were struggling to accomplish a two-turn-two schedule, mostly because of aircraft upgrades at the time, and limitations with our critical maintainer career fields. Since then, we've changed our methods of risk acceptance and maintenance cultures in how we plan training. Consequently, we

Right: **A crew chief assigned to the 177th Fighter Wing, verifies flight control surface checks on an F-16D Fighting Falcon, prior to launch at Boca Chica Field, Florida.** US Air National Guard/SMSgt Andrew Moseley

An F-16C assigned to the 177th Fighter Wing after aerial refuelling with a KC-135R Stratotanker assigned to New Jersey Air National Guard's 108th Wing en route to Naval Air Station Key West, Florida. US Air National Guard/SrA Hunter Hires

Between October 18-25, 2024, the 119th Fighter Squadron, assigned to the 177th FW of the New Jersey Air National Guard, deployed to Aviano Air Base, Italy, for Operation Pegasus Dawn, hosted by the 31st FW.

Pegasus Dawn was an agile combat employment (ACE) training mission designed to support the 108th Wing's transition from the KC-135R Stratotanker to the KC-46A Pegasus.

ACE is a proactive and reactive operational scheme of manoeuvre executed within threat timelines to increase survivability while generating combat air power. The strategy is executed by complicating the enemy's targeting process, creating political and operational dilemmas for the enemy, and creating flexibility for friendly forces.

The purpose of Pegasus Dawn was to support the 108th Wing as their teams gained valuable experience with three KC-46 aircraft deployed to the US Air Forces in Europe theatre, while integrating the aircraft and airmen into their existing systems and areas of responsibility. Pilots with the 119th FS completed daily missions, to provide relevant ACE experience for the new tanker crews. Primarily as receivers to ensure the basic aerial refuelling systems were operational.

Major Timothy Mann, F-16 pilot and director of flying with the 119th FS said: "We received fuel from them on the trans-Atlantic flight and conducted aerial refuelling with them each day of this deployment. We conducted a mix of offensive counter air (OCA) and defensive counter air missions with the 108th Wing and additional F-16s from the 555th Fighter Squadron based at Aviano." Crew chiefs assigned to the 177th Aircraft Maintenance Squadron (AMXS) serviced the F-16 aircraft and undertook maintenance activities outside of their typical Air Force Specialty Code. Explaining the scenario, Lieutenant Colonel Jessica Lewis, 177th AMXS commander said: "We had structural shop airmen assisting with replacing liquid oxygen and marshalling jets, and engine shop airmen assisting with tyre changes. We're performing aircraft maintenance with a smaller footprint which increases our flexibility for any future fight to come."

Mann said: "This week's partnership proves that the flying units of the New Jersey ANG can operate almost autonomously. It shows that our state and its airmen can organically deploy personnel, equipment, and airpower around the world with little to no outside support."

wholeheartedly in the ACE concept but there are risks that we take into a combat environment, which are not the same risks that we accept on a day-to-day training operation. So, we continue to train our young airmen and pilots and maintainers to be able to identify the risks that could potentially happen in a combat scenario, while trying to build the ACE concept as a mindset in all day-to-day training."

Combat Archer

In January 2023, airmen, and aircraft from the 177th FW deployed to Tyndall Air Force Base, Florida to participate in Air Combat Command's Combat Archer air-to-air Weapons System Evaluation Program (WSEP).

Pilots, maintainers, and support staff launched and recovered 150 sorties during the training which tests and evaluates multiple areas of operations, including weapons loading, missile employment, and aerial gunnery.

Long, then commander of the 119th Fighter Squadron, said: "One of the training goals is to familiarise the pilot to weapons deployment in

the strength of the air force supply chain system but cannibalizing parts or using suitable substitutions are two alternative options for sourcing unavailable parts.

Deployment

In the days when the 177th was gained by and assigned to Aerospace Defense Command and solely tasked with the defence of the United States, the wing made no overseas deployments. After the Aerospace Defense Command was inactivated, the 177th's gaining command became Tactical Air Command, and by 1994, the wing re-equipped with Block 25 F-16s with multi-role capability. This changed the wing's ability to deploy, and it has been regularly tasked with overseas deployments ever since.

Most recently, the 177th FW deployed to the US Central Command (CENTCOM) area of responsibility (AOR) in 2021, participated in Air Combat Command's Combat Archer air-to-air Weapon Systems Evaluation Program at Tyndall Air Force Base, Florida, and Exercise Red Flag at Nellis Air Force Base in March 2023. The Jersey Devils returned to the US CENTCOM AOR in 2023 capping off a busy year for an ANG unit with a lot of part-time guardsmen in addition to standing alert. Commenting, Long said:

"It was a heavy lift for us, but in true Jersey Devils spirit, we got the job done."

Last October, the 177th FW deployed to Aviano Air Base, Italy, for an ACE training event called Operation Pegasus Dawn. Outlining the event, Miles said: "Our sister unit, the 108th Wing based at McGuire Air Force Base is transitioning to the KC-46, so the deployment to Aviano provided an opportunity to drag fighters across the ocean, complete training overseas, and then redeploy home.

"Initially, it started as a support commitment to the 108th Wing, but we always want to get training accomplished. We focused on manning the deployment to Aviano with the smallest footprint we could take, having sufficient people and maintenance equipment to be able to operate and sustain fighter operations for several days at an overseas base. That was our overarching objective. We also completed a lot of upgrade training for the maintainers and the pilots while flying with F-16s assigned to the 31st Fighter Wing. We stopped at RAF Mildenhall on the redeployment home, stayed there for one night and continued home to New Jersey the following day."

Rounding up the discussion about the ACE paradigm, Cooper said: "We believe

Below: **An F-16C Fighting Falcon from the 177th Fighter Wing receives fuel from a KC-135R Stratotanker assigned to New Jersey Air National Guard's 108th Wing.** US Air National Guard/SrA Hunter Hires

Above: **F-16C 87-265/AC takes off from Atlantic City Air National Guard Base.** US Air National Guard/SrA Hunter Hires

combat, something that very few pilots experience more than once in their career. One of the aspects that makes Combat Archer unique is that pilots can employ live weapons, preparing them for that feeling of the missile or bomb coming off the jet."

Commenting on Combat Archer, Cooper said: "Because of our alert mission, we always have aircraft loaded with live missiles, so our folks are pretty adept at loading lives on aircraft. Combat Archer ensures that maintainers can load the weapons correctly, and for pilots, WSEP builds confidence that the aircraft will operate as it should, the missile station communicates with the aircraft, and the missile will come off the launch rail as it should. It also provides an opportunity for a pilot to put their understanding of tactics, techniques, and procedures into practise with a live fire shot. It's a pretty big deal. Ten, mostly young pilots shot missiles; we usually prioritise pilots who have never shot missiles.

Below:**F-16C 87-346/AC seen on the taxiway at an air base in the US Central Command's area of responsibility.** US Air National Guard

JERSEY JERK

F-16C 86-309 assigned to the 119th Fighter Squadron is painted with a coloured tail and wears the name Jersey Jerk in honour of Major General Donald Strait, a New Jersey Air National Guard ace who initially served as a P-47N Thunderbolt pilot with the 356th Fighter Group in World War Two. At the time Strait named his P-47N aircraft the Jersey Jerk. He had wanted to use Jersey Bounce, but that name was already taken. Initially reluctant to include the word Jerk in the name of his plane, he relented after his crew chief told him: "Sir, let me tell you why we want to name it that. Any guy that would take off in a single engine airplane, cross the North Sea in the wintertime and take a chance of getting his ass shot off by the Luftwaffe or by anti-aircraft fire has got to be a jerk."

Strait went on to command the Jersey Devils and became the commander of the entire New Jersey Air National Guard. He retired as a two-star general.

"We pride ourselves in our maintenance, and we had a 99.9% success rate in all the categories evaluated which takes dozens of maintainers to make happen. Combat Archer is invaluable training to us. When the maintainers watch the aircraft come back with nothing on the rail, that's a really great experience for them. One cool tradition we follow is to allow the maintainers to keep the missile release rings.

"The WSEP programme is essentially mandatory for all air force fighter squadrons, with some wiggle room, but we don't control our participation."

Discussing the training requirements in preparation for a deployment, Long said: "There are all kinds of training requirements for each deployment location, for the mission, and for individuals. Everybody has specific training to be combat ready. Participation in a WSEP, Red, Green or Silver Flag are training exercises that enable us to be

Above: **New Jersey Air National Guard's 119th Expeditionary Fighter Squadron arrived in the US Central Command's area of responsibility in late 2023.** US Air National Guard

Left: **A maintainer marshals an F-16C during Operation Pegasus Dawn at Aviano Air Base, Italy, on October 22, 2024.** US Air National Guard/ SrA Darion Boyd

considered ready for combat. We conduct spin-up training ahead of whichever exercise we're tasked to attend."

CENTCOM Deployment

During its last deployment to the CENTCOM AOR, the 119th Expeditionary Fighter Squadron completed a no notice real-world combat ACE. Explaining the event, Long said: "We had less than 24 hours from notification to execution which was complicated because the aircraft we had to move were not at the main operating base. So, in 24 hours, we had to recover aircraft to the main operating base where our maintainers took about three hours to drop some stores and load missiles, bombs, bullets, and prep the aircraft to complete an ACE mission. Pilots then flew to an alternate location and stood up combat ops within 22 hours of notification. At the forward location, our pilots launched and recovered each other on combat missions because our maintainers were en route. There were a lot of moving pieces, but we did the job extremely well.

"We had six pilots at the forward base who launched each other using a system where two pilots would sleep, while other pilots would recover those airplanes and then refuel them, check the oil and the hydraulics. We weren't launching all the planes at once, so we always had extra pilots on hand to launch, recover and then check the fluids. But you can only do that for two days, so we needed the maintainers to get to the forward base. Once they arrived, they worked for 12 hours straight to keep the aircraft flying on real combat missions."

Cooper helped close down Bagram Air Base in Afghanistan and was one of the last groups of air force personnel to get out of Afghanistan in 2021. Our fighter squadron, the 119th Expeditionary Fighter Squadron, was deployed to Bagram and was the last that was meant to be deployed there. When the full evacuation order came for Afghanistan, people and aircraft were deploying to other bases. Our fighter squadron's F-16s, pilots and maintainers were scheduled to go to another location outside of Afghanistan. I volunteered to help close the base down based on previous experience. The task needed skilled people, so we asked some of the maintainers and munitions people to stay to help close down the base, which primarily involved moving things."

F-16C 86-309/AC assigned to the 119th Fighter Squadron displays the 'Jersey Jerk' flagship tail at the 177th Fighter Wing, Egg Harbor Township, New Jersey, December 5, 2024. The aircraft is dedicated to US Air Force Major General Donald Strait, a retired commander of the New Jersey Air National Guard, who flew a P-47 Thunderbolt and a P-51 Mustang of the same name.
US Air National Guard/Senior Airman Darion Boyd

DEFENDERS
OF FREEDOM

Part of the Illinois Air National Guard, the 182nd Airlift Wing based at Peoria Air National Guard Base operates a fleet of C-130H Hercules transport aircraft providing worldwide airlift capability

LOCATED IN THE plains of northern Illinois, the City of Peoria was built on manufacturing, an industrial base that continues today and includes Caterpillar. Peoria International Airport is located a few miles from the downtown area serving routes throughout the United States. It shares its runway with Illinois ANG's 182nd Airlift Wing (AW), equipped with a fleet of C-130H Hercules transport aircraft.

In the last two years, the 182nd AW along with all ANG C-130H wings, was subject to an aircraft grounding order issued by Air Mobility Command in September 2023, implemented a rectification programme, and completed a deployment to the east African nation of Djibouti.

Djibouti deployment

Discussing the east African deployment, Lieutenant Colonel Brian Rezac, director of operations 169th Airlift Squadron (AS) said: "It was this wing's first deployment to the AFRICOM theatre. For the past 20 or so years we had been working in CENTCOM, mostly in Afghanistan, and then transitioning to the Middle East.

It was a standard air land cargo lifting mission supporting the Combined Joint Task Force – Horn of Africa [CJTF – HOA] for three months. We were not chopped to AFRICOM control but US Air Forces Europe, but we still had an obligation to fulfil mission requirements for the CJTF – HOA, carrying people and supplies to

various out bases. We were assigned to the 75th Expeditionary Airlift Squadron at Camp Lemonier.

"When we first arrived, the ops tempo was relatively steady, averaging two lines per day supporting new US Army or US Marine Corps units arriving in country. It was our primary mission to get them out to various forward operating bases. Once that effort was complete, the ops tempo tailed off. Consequently, we took it upon ourselves to fly training missions with US Marines Corps KC-130Js at low-level through the mountains of Djibouti.

"We completed air drops with the French military and US Air Force pararescue jumpers to maintain their proficiency in support of the personnel recovery mission and our training. Nobody deployed to Djibouti thought that they would do any type of an air drop there let alone HALO [high-altitude, low opening] jumps, but it happened."

Providing insight of infrastructure available to 182nd AW pilots and loadmasters at Djiboutian bases, Rezac said: "Forward operating bases had asphalt runways of varying quality, but they are old air strips originally 8,000ft long, so plenty big enough for the C-130. Mogadishu, Somalia and Mombasa, Kenya, have well prepared runways, although we had to use lights to create an airfield marking pattern at Mogadishu. The authorities had not turned the lights back on because of construction work. Up to 5,000ft of the strip was prepared by civil engineering teams so they were safe for landing operations by all the assets going in there. The rest of the pavement was unusable; we could taxi over it, but you wouldn't want to land the aircraft on it.

"We were the only US Air Force C-130 unit in Djibouti, operating as the 75th Expeditionary Airlift Squadron, colloquially known as the 'Rogues', and part of the 449th Air Expeditionary Group, which falls under the Air Mobility Command's 618th Air Operations Center. Despite being the only air force C-130 unit in country, that didn't restrict us to hauling only air force cargo; we hauled stuff for every service, a lot of civilians, lots of money, contractors, and people from three letter agencies. It depended on what was required to be moved, and the operating environment, which was relatively permissive. That said, we knew there were various threats out there through our intelligence briefings.

"Radar services are essentially non-existent in that part of the world, so you really have to follow the ICAO [International Civil Aviation Organization] conventions and the rules that are in place, and be cognizant of radio communications, listening to other airplanes, co-ordinating with the C2 [command and control] agencies, using TCAS [Traffic Alert and Collision Avoidance System] for situational awareness of where other airplanes are, and a lot of position reporting. You must step back and revert to things that you learned back in pilot training that are designed to keep you safe. We would sequence in with civilian and other military aircraft flying into some of those airports. There were a few times when we had to manoeuvre to avoid other airplanes that may not have been following the rules."

The 182nd aircrews flew numerous missions with one more notable than others, as Rezac explained: "We formed a task force to perform a specialised fuelling operation [SFO] at Camp Simba, a forward operating base near Manda Bay in south-eastern Kenya. The camp was running low on supplies, so we used two airplanes, crews, and shuttled fuel from Mombasa up to Manda Bay. We were able to deliver about 150,000 gallons of Jet A1 fuel, which enabled the base to remain operational for about a 15-day period until barges and other methods of delivery arrived.

Below: Airmen with the 182nd Aircraft Maintenance Squadron de-ice a C-130H Hercules at Peoria in preparation for departure to Washington DC to transport airmen from the Illinois National Guard for the 60th presidential inauguration. US Air National Guard/MSgt Lealan Buehrer

Soldiers and Airmen with the Illinois National Guard board a C-130H Hercules at Peoria bound for the US capital in support of security operations for the presidential inauguration on January 20, 2025.
US Air National Guard/MSgt Lealan Buehrer

Airmen assigned to the 182nd AW board a C-130 Hercules bound for Germany for exercise Air Defender 2023.
US Air National Guard/SSgt Paul Helmig

"The situation was caused by flooding. The one road leading to the base was completely washed out. It took us about seven days to set up and run through the approval system to practise the capability, which up until then, we had only completed in a training scenario during the previous three years, Djibouti was our first time doing SFO for real, it was a forward air refuelling point operation.

"Our loadmasters worked behind the airplane for 30 minutes at a time, getting blasted with hot engine exhaust on top of the ambient air temperature more than 150°F [65°C], while marshalling in a fuel truck, hooking up the hose and defueling gas out of the airplane. They did an amazing job. We called it Task Force Torch, our local radio callsign, which relates back to the Native American heritage around Peoria and the state of Illinois.

"During our AFRICOM deployment work-up we focused on making sure that everybody was qualified and proficient in the specialised fuelling operation capability, which was relatively new for us. We also trained to qualify for Airfield Marking Pattern-4 [AMP-4] operations, which is the ability to land at a completely blacked out strip. Normally, when we're doing landing zone work, we have lights set up, but in a third world nation, there may not be any lighting out there. We developed a training plan for how we would get everybody qualified, and how we would train to it, and then employ landing without any markings or lightings on a surface.

"There's a couple of different types of AMP. Normally, we practice to AMP-3 markings which involves a 60 x 500ft box with a trailing edge light at the end, a method that is particularly relevant to the USCENTCOM AOR. AMP-4 involves no markings, so you must find the strip and put the airplane down. We completed our initial qualifications at Decatur airport where the airport staff turned off all the lights on each of the runways and we practised landings to build on foundational skills, and then AMP-4.

"We also trained to Combat Offload Method C procedures that enable a controlled offload of single or multiple pallets with minimal taxiway space and no external equipment or support required. The pallet or pallets slide off the ramp as the aircraft inches forward. Method C is very similar to the way we already conducted offloads with a couple of minor differences."

Commenting on the deployment from a maintenance perspective, Technical Sergeant Richard Dennis, a crew chief with the 182nd Maintenance Squadron, said: "It was manageable, a good tempo, and an opportunity to get immersion training completed for our part-time folks, most of whom had not previously deployed. We flew a lot of operations and experienced operational training."

Global Force Management

Discussing tasking issue to the 182nd AW, Colonel Brandon Retherford, commander 182nd Operations Group said: "Global Force Management is the process Air Mobility Command [AMC] uses to constantly allocate forces to accomplish the airlift requirements of the US Air Force around the world. There's an Air National Guard or Air Force Reserve unit responsible for some of the deployed global force requirements all the time. We've pivoted from Afghanistan to AFRICOM for the foreseeable future with a force shared by Air National Guard and Air Force Reserve C-130 units deployed on a routine rotation that's planned well in advance. Our role is tactical airlift at the highest calling, performing airlift in direct combat.

Below: **Two C-130H Hercules from the 182nd Airlift Wing and a German Air Force A400M from Air Transport Wing 62 parked next to each other on the Advanced Airlift Tactics Training Center flightline during phase 2 of Exercise Proptoberfest at Fort Huachuca in Sierra Vista, Arizona, on September 6, 2024.** USANG/A1C Noah Hardin

"The only time we're tasked non-voluntarily as a wing is for global force tasking to Africa. Most of the time our tasking comes from the National Guard Bureau to support a sizable training network, either airlift to get from point A to point B, or more frequently, on what we call JAATT or Joint Airborne Air Transportability Training. JAATT is a programme designed to provide airborne training in a joint environment offering each service an opportunity to jointly develop tactics, knowledge, and procedures, and increase proficiency in airdrop, assault landing, and mobility operations. A JAATT mission involves extensive co-ordination, planning, and preparation to derive the maximum joint training benefit attainable."

Explaining further, Captain Joe Haubenreiser, aircrew chief with the 182nd AW said: "We serve as the jump platform for national guard and active-duty airborne units to accomplish jump training.

Above: **A loadmaster observes the propellers of a C-130 Hercules assigned to the 182nd Airlift Wing before its flight from Wunstorf Air Base, Germany during exercise Air Defender 2023.** US Air National Guard/ SSgt Paul Helmig

"The mission leans towards personnel generation to provide manpower for natural disaster relief and flood response, completing tasks like filling sandbags and helping people move; true citizen airmen roles."

Despite the variety of tasks undertaken by the 182nd AW, the wing does conduct a specialised role, as Retherford explained: "That's why we put extra focus on the combat airlift role, paying attention to high intensity training for counter threat tactics. We've invested heavily in the culture of the US Air Force Weapons School and have several weapons officers from the course who introduced the tactics and procedures they learned at the weapons school into our local and exercise training. Missouri Air National Guard's 139th AW based at St Joseph has run the C-130H Weapons Instructor Course since the active-duty air force divested the H-model. The course is run in co-operation with the 29th Weapons Squadron based at Little Rock Air Force Base, Arkansas."

Discussing home station operations, Retherford said: "When we are not deployed, our job is to train and develop people to be ready to deploy for both the full-time and the part-time force; we're probably 80% part-time, 20% full-time. We run a deliberate flying training schedule throughout every week of every month and not just during the monthly weekend and annual two-week drills.

"We can't train all of them on the same day; we established a building block method of training that starts with basic proficiency leading to local tactical proficiency to scenario-based training to TDY [temporary duty] training such

Left: **C-130H aircraft from the 182nd Airlift Wing, a C-130E from the Polish Air Force's 33rd Air Base, Poland, and a C-130J Super Hercules from the 37th Airlift Squadron based at Ramstein Air Base, Germany, during Aviation Detachment Rotation 23-4.** US Air National Guard/ Senior Airman Avery Litton

Left: **C-130H 46701 assigned to Illinois Air National Guard 182nd Airlift Wing lands at Powidz Air Base, Poland during Aviation Detachment Rotation 23-4.** US Air National Guard/SrA Avery Litton

Air Defender

as a Red Flag large force exercise. Our 'bread and butter' is at the baseline of that pyramid. Most of our flying is local training flights to places like Jackson, Mississippi."

As the chief of aircrew, Haubenreiser runs the office responsible for developing and facilitating the training. "My office works with our tactics office and the current operations office, which schedule missions to ensure we are training to the appropriate things. The schedulers set up those events, anything from local training sorties, guard lifts moving equipment for other guard units, or flying with the other services for air drops or parachutist jumps.

"We also manage upgrade training, ensuring that aircrew are progressing in their career and making sure they have the resources they need to progress from pilot to aircraft commander, flight lead, and instructor. At that stage, if a pilot is interested in attending the weapons school, we meet with representatives from the 29th Weapon Squadron to determine [what] our candidate needs to be teed up on before they submit their application to the school. If they're accepted, we then facilitate what they need before they head to St Joseph. The six-month course will take them to different training events, ultimately culminating at Nellis Air Force Base for the weapons school integration [WSINT] and graduation."

Back in June 2023, the 182nd AW participated in the big NATO exercise called Air Defender, in fact its wing leaders volunteered to take the C-130 and mobility lead for the event. An assigned weapons officer planned and co-ordinated the entirety of the tactical airlift mission and lead the integration between the primary partner nations Germany [A400], Romania [C-27], and Poland [C-130]. Over 440 airmen from nine different C-130H and C-130J units from Arkansas, Delaware, Georgia, Kentucky, Minnesota, Missouri, Nevada, Texas, and Wyoming participated.

Air Defender proved to be a mobility challenge more than a fighter challenge, because of the work required to get everyone and everything to Germany and back home again. Looking for subject matter experts in mobility, the National Guard Bureau contacted the 182nd AW, resulting in Retherford being selected to lead the operations centre at the German headquarters.

Retherford described Air Defender as a different exercise compared to most. "Usually when we partner with another nation for an exercise, we lead the whole thing. In this case, Germany led the exercise. We were the supporting force. On the live days, German subject matter experts led each of the vulnerability periods and the German command centre

Above: **Illinois Air National Guard and Polish Air Force C-130s parked on the flightline at Powidz Air Base, Poland, during Aviation Detachment Rotation 23-4 in September 2023.** US Air National Guard/ SrA Avery Litton

undertook all the co-ordination. We were a force provider to amplify the effects they wanted to achieve, something the guard does for the active-duty air force."

According to the tactical operations centre at Wunstorf Air Base, the 182nd AW oversaw 345 C-130 missions

Right: **Two C-130H Hercules assigned to the 182nd Airlift Wing at Powidz Air Base, Poland. Note the lack of colour tail markings on the aircraft furthest from camera.** US Air National Guard/SrA Avery Litton

amounting to 351 hours of tactical airlift missions which included transporting 1,308 personnel, and more than 1.3 million pounds of cargo during the exercise. Airmen with the 182nd AW were also involved in C-130 maintenance, fuelling of various types of aircraft, and providing connectivity through cyber communication operations systems.

Tactical Airlift and ACE

Discussing the tactical airlift mission, Retherford said: "As a C-130 operator, our tactical airlift mission is directly tied to the end user. We deliver cargo from the strategic hubs to smaller fields in conflict-ridden areas directly to the end user. In high-level exercises, people are surprised with what we can do with the C-130H; we don't need a lot of support from different entities and can accomplish a lot on our own. For example, we can land on a 3,000 x 60ft strip with 40,000lb of cargo or air drop up to 42,000lb of cargo using the low altitude low velocity method originally designed to drop ammunition, water, food to forward operating bases in Afghanistan. We can accurately drop bundles, execute an engine-running offload to quickly deliver equipment into small fields without the need for a lot of support equipment. We're usually first in and last out of such places."

Above: **A C-130H assigned to the 182nd Airlift Wing fitted with NP2000 propellors.** US Air National Guard/SrA Avery Litton

All combat-coded air force units now practise operations in accordance with the Agile Concept Employment (ACE) concept of operations. According to Retherford: "The C-130 is probably one of the most suitable airplanes to execute ACE; it carries a decent amount of gas so we can offload some fuel in specialized fuelling operations and deliver cargo. We can deliver maintenance packages and weapons support for A-10s landing on a Michigan state highway conducting integrated combat turns. Ahead of the A-10s' arrival, a C-130 landed on the highway, parked to the side, and offloaded the maintenance package.

Once on the ground, the A-10s were refuelled and rearmed, then took off followed by the C-130.

"One of the main aspects of the ACE concept of operations is the use of multi-capable airmen, those that can perform other roles in addition to those specific to their AFSC code. Retherford believes the ANG is well postured for the concept of the multi-capable airman. "As a part-time force, a traditional guardsman who might be a firefighter in their civilian job but works in maintenance for the wing. ACE fits our skill set. We're used to operating on our own and don't have as many requirements to facilitate turning a C-130 and getting it ready to go. We can bring a small contingent of maintainers and operate solely on one airplane.

"We worked with the F-35-equipped 115th Fighter Wing based at Madison, Wisconsin. F-35s landed at a small regional airfield where we had flown a maintenance team to prior to the jet's arrival. The maintainers turned the jets for a follow-on mission, which is a good example of our wing executing its mission as a facilitator for ACE operations.

"Command relationships are one aspect of operations that the C-130 community is used to. We forward deploy and then belong to the theatre combatant commander that we're supporting. Whereas the C-5, C-17, and tanker communities remain under the command of AMC, no matter where they are on the globe. For the ACE concept to be inherently effective, it must be wholly and entirely distributed; you can't hang on to the command and control all the way back to AMC, whereas we always chop to the theatre we're going to operate from, AMC doesn't even know we're gone."

Above:
Loadmasters assigned to the 169th Airlift Squadron practise winching heavy equipment on and off a C-130H Hercules to ensure mission readiness and proficiency.
US Air National Guard/SrA Avery Litton

Below: **A C-130H on the Peoria apron at sunrise.**
US Air National Guard/SSgt Lealan Buehrer

Propellor Checks

When a propeller of a US Marine Corps KC-130T came loose in flight on over Mississippi July 10, 2017, 16 people onboard were killed. The outcome of the investigations and maintenance reviews found there were hairline fractures beginning to form in the root of the base of each propeller blade. Maintainers had to perform off-wing eddy current inspection and validate the barrel hubs that hold the propellers together.

Some propellors were found to be serviceable and others were found to be deficient. A subsequent process to re-label a new serial number on the serviceable examples instituted a defect that was even more risky. Consequently, the entire ANG fleet was grounded and manufacturing production to recover from the discovery took 18 months. During the year leading up to the AFRICOM deployment, the 182nd Operations Group struggled to get much flying.

Contingency Response

The 182nd AW maintains the highest mission capable rates in the USAF for the C-130H, which Retherford says is the result of the relationship between aircrew and maintainers. "As a culture, it's distinctly unheard of in its efficiency and optimisation which allows them to be able to turn aircraft and fly when planned.

"In addition to that, we're gaining a new contingency response group, under a new concept in the Air National Guard to address the near peer threat in the Asian theatre. Contingency Response Groups [CRGs] were originally activated in Air Mobility Command manned by AFSCs from across an entire wing. A CRG is an expeditionary resource to forward deploy and open up a mobility air base, whether it's on a road or an airfield, and optimizing it for operations. The overarching mission of a CRG is to provide highly specialised airmen who are capable of rapidly deploying to quickly open airfields and establish, expand, sustain, and co-ordinate air mobility operations. The US Air Force has elected to decommission Air Support Operations Groups in favour of CRGs."

C-130 Maintenance

Technical Sergeant Richard Dennis works for the 182nd Maintenance Squadron as a crew chief performing in-depth inspections (referred to as ISO), with the aircraft housed inside a hangar, for three to five weeks. That entails aircraft being stripped down to allow access to the structure and systems to ensure they meet all inspection criteria.

While deployed to Djibouti, Dennis worked with a flight-line crew chief conducting pre-flight inspections and periodical inspections, to ensure any discrepancies found within that aircraft are rectified before take-off, work that may involve back shops to address set issues or discrepancies requiring specialised skills.

Dennis and his ISO crew chief colleagues support their crew chiefs assigned to the 182nd Aircraft Maintenance Squadron to support launching missions on the flight line.

Right: **Airmen assigned to the 375th Operations Support Squadron's Survival, Evasion, Resistance, and Escape unit in a static line jump from a C-130H assigned to the 182nd Airlift Wing.** US Air Force/A1C Chad Gorecki

Dennis previously worked for the 193rd Aircraft Maintenance Squadron at Harrisburg, Pennsylvania, maintaining the EC-130J. His transition from the newer J-model to an older model is different. Dennis said: "It makes no huge difference, because maintainers are trained to address every fault that we can possibly find, even if a computer doesn't tell you to. During our J-model training we were told not to rely on a computerised health monitoring system. It's very convenient to have an airplane that can advise you of the issues but over 30 years of service, all issues with the C-130H have been realised and our experienced maintainers, and to a degree their younger colleagues, can appropriately address them."

Highlighting some of the reasons for the high mission capable rates achieved at the Peoria-based wing, Retherford said: "The guard benefits from a low turnover rate of maintainers. We have dedicated crew chiefs who have worked on these

aircraft for a considerable amount of their career and take a lot of pride in the airplane they're in charge of.

"Several years ago, our maintenance team took a deep dive into process improvement and analysed the ISO process, and reoriented some work

schedules, even though we operate a single shift. They sequenced which maintainers came in at what time, based on the requirements of the specific ISO inspection cards. Consequently, they reduced an ISO inspection from 30 days, down to an average of 18 days.

Right: **A C-130H assigned to the 182nd Air Wing takes off from Young Landing Zone at Fort McCoy, Wisconsin.** US Air National Guard/MSgt Todd Pendleton

Above: **A 182nd AW C-130H on a local training sortie near Peoria on April 30, 2024.** US Air National Guard/ MSgt Lealan Buehrer

Left: **A 182nd AW C-130H and a 126th ARW KC-135R Stratotanker fly a formation near Springfield, Illinois, home of the 183rd Wing. The three wings make up the Illinois Air National Guard.** US Air National Guard/MSgt Ryan Lane

Below: **C-130H 46701 assigned to the 182nd AW on a training flight over the flat vast land of Illinois.** US Air National Guardane

As a result, aircraft availability has gone through the roof. For 14 of the last 16 years, this wing has held the highest mission capability rate in AMC.

"The 182nd Maintenance Squadron primarily performs back shop and flightline support to include structural, avionics, hydraulic, electrical, environmental, fuels, and fabrication. Additionally, we conduct scheduled home station check (HSC) inspections, Non-Destructive Inspections (NDI) which involves X-rays and liquid penetrant tests, and support to Aerospace Ground Equipment (AGE) and munitions storage facilities. By comparison, the Aircraft Maintenance Squadron, is responsible for aircraft generation, with one specialized work centre focused on launching and recovering aircraft.

"The individual back shops each conduct a specialised type of maintenance. Avionics includes guidance and control, communication, datalinks, and navigations, and avionics components in the fuel cell that filter up to the gauges that the pilot sees on the dash for the aircraft's fuel status. Electrical and environmental maintain and repair the

wiring and electrical components, cabin pressurisation to engine control, and the fire suppression system. Propulsion takes care of engines and propellers. Fabrication consists of metals technology, the design and fabrication of metal components. Sheet metal cuts and welds metal, and structures conducts non-destructive inspection.

"Crew chiefs assigned to the 62nd-Aircraft-Maintenance-Squadron [AMXS] are all purpose general maintainers working on the flight line. We try to rotate the back shop crew chiefs with the flight line so that everybody learns the inner workings of everything required inside their career field. Crew chiefs with the AMXS deal with the flight engineers assigned to the ops group and the aerial porters who load and unload the aircraft and check the weight and balance of pallets loaded on the aircraft.

"Propulsion is currently the busiest work centre because while trying to meet the daily flight schedule, it must address any issues that pop up with the new NP2000 propellers and forecast other modifications coming down the pipeline."

On September 14, 2023, the USAF announced it had tentatively selected the 103rd AW in Connecticut, the 120th Airlift Wing in Montana, the 133rd AW in Minnesota, and the 182nd AW in Illinois to convert from ageing C-130H Hercules aircraft to the more advanced C-130J Super Hercules. Each unit will receive eight C-130Js but no timeframe for the change was given.

Commenting on the news, Retherford said: "Our conversion to the C-130J will start in 2026. It ensures the wing's continued existence because that's always a concern in the guard and reserve, especially when the active-duty component transitions to a different airframe. There's always a concern that you're flying something that may get divested and then face an uncertain future of the wing. We're going to lose two crew positions – the navigator and flight engineer – which are not employed on the C-130J. However, those folks will have opportunities to continue their career on the airplane or moving to different jobs."